The Nine Steps to a *Complete* ESTATE PLAN

View Legal

Matthew Burgess

Patrick Ellwood

National Library of Australia Cataloguing-in-Publication entry (pbk)

Author: Burgess, Matthew, author.

Title: The nine steps to a complete estate plan / Matthew Burgess; interior book layout by Otto Dimitrijevics.

ISBN: 9781925181159 (paperback)

Subjects: Estate planning—Popular works.
Trusts and trustees—Popular works.
Future interests—Popular works.
Probate law and practice—Popular works.
Estates (Law)—Popular works.

Other Authors/Contributors: Dimitrijevics, Otto, book designer.

Dewey Number: 332.024016

Important disclaimer

This book covers legal and technical issues in a general way. It is not designed to express opinions on specific cases. This book is intended for information purposes only and should not be regarded as legal advice. Further advice should be obtained before taking action on any issue dealt with in this publication.

Table of Contents

Introduction

Matthew Burgess, Patrick Ellwood, Naomi Arnold and Tara Lucke are co-founders, of View Legal.

Having previously founded Australia's first virtual law firm as a wholly owned subsidiary of one of the country's leading independent law firms, View Legal is results focused and passionate about delivering new solutions in a way that aligns with their 'SPS' – service and price satisfaction – guarantee.

As authors, Patrick and Matthew are recognised as experts in their fields, and constantly create innovative strategies for the growth, management and protection of wealth.

They are widely published across a range of topics including:

1. The Seven Key Aspects of Testamentary Trusts.
2. The Four Foundations of Business Succession.
3. Seven Essential Blue Journal Articles.
4. Inside Stories – the complete collection of blog posts (2010-2013)

Acknowledgements

This book has been based on material published by a number of leading lawyers at View Legal and, historically, the firm McCullough Robertson Lawyers. The assistance of all involved is gratefully acknowledged.

Glossary of key terms

Administrator: The person who is appointed by the Court to administer a will where there is no executor power under the will.

Beneficiary: A person who receives a benefit under a will, or from a trust.

Capital Gain: A capital gain occurs when the amount received on the disposal of an asset is greater than the cost base.

Capital gains tax (CGT): The tax imposed on assets acquired after 19 September 1985 that has a market value on disposal greater than its cost base.

Codicil: A document that amends an existing will.

Cost base: The cost base of an asset is generally the purchase price, plus the incidental expenses of acquisition and the costs of any improvements.

Deceased Estate: This is made up of all of the assets owned by the deceased when they die.

De facto spouse: A person will be a de facto spouse of a testator if they are not legally married and are living together as a couple on a genuine domestic basis.

Discretionary Trust: A trust where the trustee has the discretion to determine who should receive income and capital from a trust – from a defined class of beneficiaries, and when that distribution should occur. Often referred to as a 'family trust'.

Executor: The person appointed by a will to administer the deceased estate. The executor holds all of the assets of the deceased until they are distributed in accordance with the will.

Family Provision Legislation: This legislation gives certain eligible people the right to claim a share of the deceased estate, despite the provisions of the will. The purpose of this legislation is to ensure that families and other dependants of the deceased are adequately provided for out of the estate.

Fixed Trust: The beneficiary in a fixed trust has a specific entitlement to a share of the trust assets and income from those assets. The trustee does not have discretion to determine who should benefit.

Guardian: The person nominated by a will to care for infant children if both parents die. While a nomination of a guardian under a will is given significant weight, the appointment can be reviewed by the Family Court, on application from a concerned interested party.

Inter vivos trust: This is a trust that is set up by a person during their lifetime ('inter' meaning during and 'vivos' meaning life).

Intestate: A person who dies without a will is called an 'Intestate', and an intestacy is created by their failure to dispose of their assets. A partial intestacy can occur when some, but not all, of the assets are disposed of by will.

Joint tenancy: This occurs where assets are held jointly by two or more people. Upon the death of one of the joint tenants, their share of the property passes automatically to the other joint tenant(s) (the right of survivorship).

Personal representative: General term for 'executor' and 'trustee' or the person appointed to administer the estate. Often the term 'legal personal representative' (LPR) is used.

Principal: The person who has the power to appoint and remove the trustee of a trust (also referred to as an 'appointor' and 'nominator').

Probate: An order from the Supreme Court, which gives the executor authority to administer the estate in accordance with the terms of the will.

Settlor: A settlor is a person who establishes a trust, usually by giving a nominal amount to the trustee. For TT, the settlor is the will-maker.

SMSF: Is a self-managed super fund.

Tax Act: Means either the Income Tax Assessment Act 1936 or 1997, as the case may be.

Spouse: A person's spouse is their husband or wife. For succession law purposes, a person whose marriage has been dissolved will no longer be a spouse.

Tenancy in common: This occurs where assets are held by two or more people, in equal or unequal shares, but not jointly. Each tenant-in-common owner can individually sell, or otherwise dispose of, their share of the property.

Testamentary trust (TT): Is a trust that is established by some's will and does not come into effect until their death. Often a TT will be crafted along the lines of a family discretionary trust, including so that any discretionary aspect is limited to lineal descendant (or 'bloodline') beneficiaries.

Testator: The person who makes the will – also referred to as 'will-maker'.

Trust deed: The rules of a trust are set out in the trust deed. For TTs, the will is the trust deed.

Trustee: The person who is the legal owner of the property in the trust. The trustee holds and administers the property of the trust for the benefit of the beneficiaries, in accordance with the terms of the trust.

Trust property: The property that is held by the trustee of the trust, in accordance with the provisions of the trust deed.

Introduction

IN RECENT YEARS, the need for effective structuring of business and personal assets has been brought into sharp focus for high net worth individuals and business owners.

Fundamental changes to the taxation regime, the vast amounts of wealth accumulated within superannuation funds and the increasing tendency for both business and personal relationships to be relatively short term, as opposed to life long, have meant that traditional estate planning has been revolutionised.

A significant factor to note in the changing face of estate planning is the transfer of wealth from Australia's 'baby boomer' generation. Statistically, this segment of the population is by far the wealthiest and best educated in Australia's history, and consequently far more sophisticated estate planning strategies are being developed in order to minimise the ability for wealth to be attacked by creditors, former spouses, business associates and (in some instances) disgruntled beneficiaries.

While tax effective strategies incorporating complex will arrangements and TTs continue to be of relevance, recent developments in estate planning have been more focused on the protection of underlying wealth.

In particular, additional structures are now being utilised, in conjunction with wills, to ensure that wealth passes efficiently to the intended recipients and that the transfer takes place at the intended time. Often, in deciding on an estate plan, the desire to ensure a suitable tax outcome needs to be balanced against a desire to ensure that assets are protected from family disputes, spendthrift beneficiaries and creditors.

Asset protection strategies and the use of special purpose trusts are important issues to consider in estate planning, particularly where potential beneficiaries are in occupations, professional practice or in business, or where there is a risk that a personal relationship of a beneficiary might degenerate in the future. Potential beneficiaries that fall into any of these 'at risk' categories will be exposed to losing assets, unless appropriate structures are put in place.

The difficulty in many estate-planning exercises is that serious attempts to devise and implement a plan are often not made until some 'triggering event' stimulates action. Often the triggering event is itself an issue that might jeopardise the ability to implement appropriate strategies – for example, financial or matrimonial misfortune or life threatening illness.

Given that the first wave of the baby boomer generation is now nearing 70, it is likely that the increased focus, in recent years, on appropriately structuring intergenerational wealth transfers will continue to intensify.

In this context, this book aims to provide a comprehensive guide to the core aspects of an estate-planning exercise.

Chapter 1

DEALING WITH PERSONALLY OWNED ASSETS

Wills

What is a will?

A will is a document that enables the testator to direct who is to receive assets from the estate and on what terms, after the testator's death.

A will allows the testator to appoint whomever they want as the executor – that is the person who will administer the estate following their death.

If the testator has infant children, it is possible to nominate a guardian, by the will, to ensure that the children are properly cared for.

A will can be revoked by making another will, or can be updated throughout the life of the testator.

What assets are governed by the will?

A will does not govern all the assets that the testator owns or controls, but will only govern the estate assets.

Estate assets include:

a all assets owned personally
b shares in a company
c the share of any asset owned as a tenant-in-common
d any superannuation death benefit or life insurance policy proceeds paid to the estate
e an interest in any partnership assets, unless agreed otherwise
f the right to recover any funds owed
g any rights held under any contract.

Estate assets do not include:

a assets owned as a joint tenant
b assets held in a trust

c assets owned by a company
d superannuation death benefits or life insurance policy proceeds paid directly to a beneficiary.

A brief summary of the main types of assets that do not pass pursuant to a person's will are set out below.

Asset type	**Control**	**Documents regulating**
Joint Tenancy (as opposed to tenants in common)	Survivor	Position at law
Superannuation (binding nomination)	Member within 3 years of death	Valid binding nomination
Superannuation (no binding nomination)	Fund trustee post death	Trust Deed or Terms of Pension
Discretionary Trust (individual trustee)	Appointor/Principal, or in the absence of both, surviving trustee. If no surviving trustee then legal personal representative of estate	Trust Deed or Trusts Act
Discretionary Trustee (corporate trustee)	Appointor/Principal, or in the absence of both, remaining directors of corporate trustee, subject to the shareholder's power to remove	Trust Deed or constitution for corporate trustee

Asset type	Control	Documents regulating
Unit Trust	As above for discretionary trusts	Ultimate benefit in trust regulated by Trust Deed and unitholdings
Private Company	Director subject to appointment by shareholders	Constitution or shareholders agreement. Transfer of shares may be pursuant to will depending on other documentation
Loan to Company or Trust	Lender or legal personal representative of Lender	Loan Agreement may override will
Business interests	Remaining business owners/trustee of will	Business Succession Agreement/Partnership Act
Life Insurance	Policy owner or nominated beneficiary	Insurance Policy

What happens to assets in the estate if the testator dies without a will?

If the testator dies without a will, the law says that their assets will be distributed to their family, as determined by a set formula, which is different in every Australian state.

To provide some general examples of the possible outcomes (bearing in mind the actual outcomes will be different in each state), if the testator dies leaving:

a their spouse, but no children, then their spouse receives the entire estate

b. their spouse and children, then their spouse receives the first $150,000 and one half of the balance of the estate (if there is one child), or one third of the balance (if there is more than one child). The testator's children share the balance of the estate equally
c. children but no spouse, then their children receive a share each, but only if they are 18 years of age or married
d. no spouse or children, then their parents will share the estate of the testator
e. no spouse, no children and no parents, then their siblings share the estate equally.

The amount received by each person will depend on the value of the estate and whether any other beneficiaries are entitled to the assets of the testator.

If the testator does not have any family members who qualify, then the assets may pass to the Government.

It is necessary that someone apply to the Court to be appointed as the administrator, to ensure that the testator's estate is properly administered. Failure to do so may result in additional time and costs to the administration of the estate.

If the testator has young children and a guardian is needed, an application to the Court might also have to be made.

Court drafted wills

One of the more fundamental developments in relation to estate planning in recent years has been the introduction, in most Australian states, of government legislation empowering courts to make wills on behalf of people who otherwise lack the capacity.

There has been an increasing number of cases in this area.

The case of *Re Matsis; Charalambous v Charalambous & Others [2012] QSC 439* is particularly interesting as it appears to be the first case that allowed a court-ordered will where the primary objective was not because the relevant incapacitated person had no will at all.

The situation was rather that the pre-existing will did not achieve the appropriate asset protection and tax planning objectives of the ultimate beneficiaries.

The case involved a businessman who had accumulated some millions of dollars of wealth and who, at some time before losing capacity to dementia, had signed an 'interim' will, which did not incorporate any TTs.

On the application of the ultimate beneficiaries, the court allowed them to introduce comprehensive TT provisions into the will as if they had been inserted before the will-maker's death.

The decision is particularly important because in the past there have been other cases where similar requests have been denied.

Arguably, the important factors here included:

a it was possible to show evidence that the will that was in place before the will-maker lost capacity was largely seen by him as an 'interim' document
b the only person who could have brought a challenge against the estate was the will-maker's daughter, who indicated in the proceedings that she was independently wealthy and had no intention of challenging the estate;
c the ultimate beneficiaries of the estate (the people bringing the application) were the will-makers' grandsons. While each of them potentially had asset protection risks, they were not aware of any potential litigation
d the change to the existing will did not alter any of the provisions, for example, in relation to executorship or any specific gifts
e while the grandsons lost direct entitlement by the inclusion of the TTs, they were still ultimately the likely potential beneficiaries via the trust structures
f the court accepted evidence that the will-maker may well have himself implemented TT provisions, had he not lost capacity.

Things to consider when making a will

There are many things to consider when making an estate plan. Some of the key questions (where applicable) include:

a Who should be the executor of the will?
b Who should be appointed to make financial, personal and medical decisions on my behalf, if there is a loss of capacity to make these decisions?
c If the first named executor or attorney is not able to act, who is appointed?
d Other than immediate family members, are there any other individuals or entities who should receive part of the estate?
e Are there any specific directions or gifts?
f In the unfortunate circumstances that all members of an immediate family die together, who should the estate pass to?
g If life spouses both die together, who will look after the children (that is, who should be the guardian)?

Executor

What role does the executor perform?

The duties of an executor are many and include:

a to supervise the funeral arrangements
b to call in the assets of the estate: this often involves applying to the Court for permission to deal with the assets under the will and collecting all assets and debts due to the estate
c to pay all outstanding debts: ideally this should be done within 12 months of the date of death, but the Court can allow a longer period if it is reasonable in the circumstances
d to invest estate funds so as to earn interest whilst the estate is being administered
e to insure the assets of the estate against fire and other risks
f to distribute the assets in accordance with the will
g to arrange the completion of tax returns for both the testator and the testator's estate.

How many executors can be appointed?

It is important that at least one executor be appointed by the will. However, it is common that a back-up or alternative executor is appointed, in case one of the named executors is unable to act, or does not wish to act.

No more than four persons may apply to the Court for permission to administer the estate.

If the executors cannot agree on the administration of the will, they will need to apply to the Court for a ruling.

What personal liability does the executor take on?

Once the executor has permission from the Court to deal with the estate, they must act promptly to collect all the assets and debts of the estate.

They may be held personally liable for any loss suffered through their neglect.

If the executor fails to invest the assets of the estate, they may be liable to pay the interest that would have gone to the beneficiaries had the assets been properly invested.

Who carries out the executor's functions if no executor is appointed?

If no executor is named in the will, it becomes necessary to apply to the Court, so that the Court can appoint someone to administer the deceased estate.

When appointing an administrator, the Court will have regard to the rights of those people who are interested in the real and personal estate of the testator.

The Court will appoint someone who has an interest in the residuary estate, but has the discretion to appoint someone else, if the circumstances warrant.

Who carries on the administration of the estate if the executor dies?

If the executor administering the estate dies, then any alternative executor appointed under the will becomes the executor of the estate.

If no alternative executor is appointed, the Court has the power to appoint an administrator to the estate.

Who should be appointed as an executor?

From a legal point of view, the only requirements when appointing an executor are that they are at least 18 years of age and of sound mind.

Careful thought must be given to the appointment of executors.

The qualities needed of an executor are generally seen to be those of honesty, business acumen and organisation.

The testator should choose someone who is likely to survive them, and someone who will carry out the discretionary aspects of the administration of the estate in accordance with the testator's wishes.

It is important that the person chosen as the executor knows and understands the responsibilities involved, and is capable of carrying them out, especially where the estate is large or complex. Any family or business pressures that might affect the executor's ability to carry out the proper administration of the estate should also be taken into account.

Executors can be family members, respected business associates, trusted friends, professional advisers or trustee companies. Where a professional executor is chosen, a commission may be payable.

What steps must be taken by the executor to gain control of the assets?

Before the executor can deal with any of the assets in the estate, they are often required to obtain probate of the will.

This is a formal procedure where the Court declares the validity of the will and confirms the appointment of the executor.

There are a number of things that must be done before the application for probate will be accepted. These include:

a locating the last will of the testator
b applying for a Tax File Number (**TFN**) for the estate, and opening an estate bank account
c advertising the intention to apply for probate, in a major newspaper in the city where the testator most recently lived
d lodging the probate application, which includes a summons, an affidavit, the original death certificate, the original will and the notice of intended application.

Once probate is granted, the executor has the power to administer the estate in accordance with the terms of the will.

Is gaining probate of the will essential?

It is not always necessary to obtain probate.

If, for example, all the assets of the deceased are owned in a joint tenancy, then the survivor automatically inherits those assets.

Life insurance companies often permit the pay out of life insurance policies, less than certain sums, without the production of probate.

Guardians

IF THE TESTATOR has infant children (under the age of 18), then they can appoint a guardian for those children, in their will. Ordinarily, a child's surviving parent will automatically be the child's guardian (even if the child was living only with the testator). However, it is important that the testator provides for circumstances in which both the child's parents were to die together.

The appointment of a guardian in a will is only a declaration of the testator's intention. The Family Court retains the ultimate power to appoint an alternative guardian if it believes it is in the best interests of the child.

Generally, a guardian has all rights and powers in respect to the welfare and upbringing of a child, such as the child's parent would have had. These include the right to have the daily care and control of the child, and the right and responsibility to make decisions concerning the child's welfare.

Who would be the guardian of a child if no appointment is made under the will?

In instances where no guardian has been appointed under the will, and there is no surviving parent, the Court can make an order appointing a guardian.

The Court will take into consideration the needs and circumstances of the child.

Can guardians be validly appointed where the parents have separated?

Where the Family Court has awarded custody to one parent and that parent subsequently dies, the surviving parent does not have an automatic right to custody of the child, although the Family Court will generally prefer to see this outcome.

The surviving parent can make an application for guardianship and custody, as can any person who has the care and control of the child at the time.

If the deceased custodial parent has appointed a guardian under their will, that guardian will have the right of custody over the surviving parent, subject to the exercise of the Court's power to appoint an alternate guardian.

Validity of wills

What is a valid will?

While the rules in each Australian state are different, generally, in order for a will to be valid, it must be signed by the testator and witnessed by two independent adult witnesses (over the age of 18 years).

Both witnesses must be present at the time when the testator signs, and also when they sign as witnesses.

If the testator is under a disability, such as a sight impairment, then the will must state that it was read aloud to the testator, and that the testator understood and approved of its contents.

The witnesses to the will must not be beneficiaries, or be related, married or engaged to be married, to a beneficiary.

What can cause a will to become invalid?

If a will is made, and the testator subsequently marries, the marriage will revoke that will, unless the will states that it is made in contemplation of the marriage.

If a will is made while the testator is married, and subsequently a divorce takes place, this can affect the will.

In many Australian states, divorce will automatically invalidate the entire will, in so far as it benefits the former spouse, unless the will specifically provides that it is made in contemplation of the divorce.

Divorce and estate planning

The impact of a relationship breakdown on any estate plan must be considered carefully.

While in many jurisdictions, a formal divorce leads to a partial revocation of an existing will, if the couple has only separated or, alternatively, if they have only had a property settlement, neither of these events impact on pre-existing wills.

Generally speaking, before a divorce takes place, there must be complete separation for 12 months following a breakdown of the relationship. On that basis, the conservative recommendation would always be to update wills and related documentation as soon as permanent separation takes place.

In most instances, particularly where the estate planning documents have been implemented in recent years, this process need neither be time consuming nor expensive.

What can cause a will to be valid but out of date?

A will is current if it takes into account all the present circumstances of the testator, such as marital status, whether there are any children, the age of those children and whether those children need to be provided for in any particular or special way.

If the testator has recently become divorced, is marrying for the second time or their financial circumstances have altered, then the will is automatically out of date and should be updated.

It is important to consider the following factors that might cause a will to be out of date, namely whether:

a the people named in the will are still alive and using the same name
b the people appointed as guardians and executors are still appropriate
c the situations or needs of any of the beneficiaries have changed
d all the assets specifically mentioned in the will are still owned by the testator
e the tax laws have changed in a way that might affect the testator's plans for the beneficiaries
f the beneficiaries are able to protect their gift from any creditors or from a Family Law dispute.

Challenges to a will

Who can challenge a deceased's will?

The Court has the power to change how an estate will be distributed if that would be necessary to achieve a 'just' result.

Generally, the following people may apply to challenge a will:

a the wife or husband of the deceased
b the de facto of the deceased at the time of death
c a former wife or husband
d a child of the deceased
e the parents of the deceased
f a person who is divorced from the deceased but who is, at the date of death, entitled to receive maintenance from the deceased.

What is the timeframe within which a challenge must be commenced?

Generally, the timeframe within which a challenge must be commenced is nine months from the date of death.

What issues does the Court consider when determining whether to uphold a challenge?

Several things are taken into consideration by the Court when hearing a challenge to a will. These include issues such as the wealth and the financial positions of the claimant and the testator, any provision that the testator had made for their spouse or children during their lifetime, and the current and future needs of the testator's spouse and children.

The Court must consider the moral obligation (or duty) that the testator had to provide for the claimant against the competing interests and needs of the beneficiaries under the will.

The Court then has the power to change how an estate will be distributed if it believes it would be necessary to achieve a just and fair result, and to ensure that those left without adequate provision are properly provided for.

Who meets the cost of a challenge?

If a claim is successful, the estate of the testator will normally have to pay all the legal costs associated with the challenge. The estate will then also have to provide the funds to the successful claimant.

If the claim is not successful, then often the estate will still pay the costs, unless the Court believes that the challenger brought the claim without proper purpose.

What can be done to prevent a challenge or minimise its impact?

If the will-maker sees the likelihood of a claim, it might be necessary to craft the will so as to provide for the likely claimant.

It is often possible to increase the value of the estate by taking out additional insurance cover to fund a gift to the potential claimant.

If there are good reasons for not including likely claimants, then it is best to document the reasons for excluding them from a will. This is often done via a separate document such as a statutory declaration or perhaps a letter of wishes (to be discussed later).

In some circumstances, it can be appropriate, prior to death, to move assets out of the testator's name into structures not regulated by the will (for example, discretionary trusts or SMSFs) to as to limit the impact of any challenge.

The CGT and stamp duty costs should be considered before any asset transfers. It is also important to note that New South Wales has legislation that limits a testator's ability to successfully avoid challenges, by moving assets pre death. Other states might introduce this legislation in the future, although in 2013 Victoria confirmed it had no intention of doing so.

Trusts

Trusts overview

A trust is, in effect, simply a legal relationship where there is:

a a legal owner of property (the 'trustee'), who
b holds the property ('trust property')
c for the benefit of others (the 'beneficiaries')
d pursuant to certain terms or rules ('trust deed').

Diagrammatically, the structure of a trust is represented as follows:

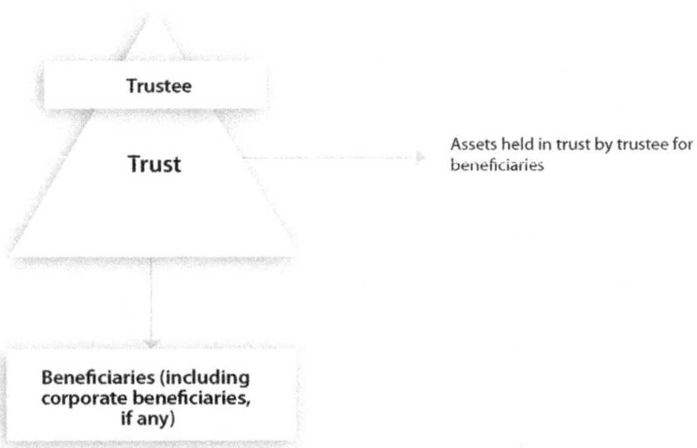

Trustee

The trustee of the trust is the legal owner of the property. The trustee will therefore have the ultimate control over the assets of the trust.

The trustee can be a company or one or more individuals. Where the trustee is a company, the directors of the company will have the day-to-day control of the trust.

As the directors are appointed by the shareholders of the company, then the shareholders have the ultimate control over the trust.

Despite this control, the shares in the trustee company will normally be worth only a nominal amount, regardless of the value of the assets in the trust that the trustee company controls.

Care must be taken, from a stamp duty perspective, in relation to shares in trustee companies. In some states a notional value can be attributed to the shares in the trustee company, based on the value of the trust assets, rather than on the value of the shares themselves.

Although the trustee is responsible for the day-to-day running of the trust, many trusts also have a '*principal*', who retains ultimate control over the trust. The principal has the ability to appoint and remove the trustee at any time, and its consent may be required to make any amendments to the trust deed.

If the trust deed does not name a principal, the existing trustee will usually have the power to appoint a new trustee.

Beneficiaries

The discretionary trust structure enables income that is earned by the trust to be distributed to the beneficiaries of the trust, in such proportions as the trustee decides.

Normally, there are numerous beneficiaries set out, including, for example, a mother and father, children and grandchildren, any brothers or sisters of any one mentioned before, any other trust in which any of these people are potential beneficiaries, and any company in which any of these people hold an interest. These people are normally referred to as '*discretionary beneficiaries*'. The idea of including a large number of discretionary beneficiaries is to allow the trustee maximum flexibility when distributing income.

The trustee has the ability to decide the proportions in which the income of the trust is distributed among these potential beneficiaries, based on what will be appropriate, given the needs of the beneficiaries and what is most tax effective in any given year.

One common strategy is to include a company as a potential beneficiary of the trust. Companies are currently taxed at a flat rate of 30%, therefore the distribution of income from the trust to the company, can be an effective strategy to limit the overall tax paid by a family group.

Normally there will be one or two people who have an expectation of receiving income from the trust. These people are commonly referred to as the '*primary beneficiaries*'.

Most trusts set out who is to be entitled to the income of the trust, if the trustee does not exercise its discretion to decide how to distribute the income. These are known as the '*default beneficiaries*'. Most trusts separately set out who are the default beneficiaries for any income that has not been distributed at the end of each year, and who are the default beneficiaries for capital upon the winding up of the trust. Often the primary beneficiaries and the default beneficiaries are the same individuals.

Trust deed

Most trusts are governed by a trust deed. This sets out how the trust must be run, what the trustees can do in running the trust and who the beneficiaries are. Discretionary trusts have been used as a tax effective asset owning vehicle for a long time. Consequently, there are large numbers of trusts, governed by trust deeds that were drafted when tax laws and trust law were significantly different.

Where a trust is established under a will (a 'testamentary' trust) the rules of the trust (or the 'trust deed') are set out in the will itself.

It is necessary to review a trust deed periodically to ensure that it allows the trustees to operate the trust in the most tax effective way.

It is also important to review the terms of the trust deed carefully with particular reference to issues such as:

a the vesting day (or ending day) of the trust. In all states other than South Australia a trust can last for a maximum period of 80 years

b whether there is a '*principal*', '*appointor*' or '*nominator*'. This person or entity has the ability to remove and appoint trustees at their total discretion

c the powers the trustee has in relation to administering the trust. For example, often trustees might not be able to grant options in relation to trust property
d the provisions that apply in the event a trustee fails to make a distribution.

Further commentary in relation to trusts is set out in Chapter 4.

What is a TT?

A testamentary trust (**TT**) is a trust established in someone's will. It comes into existence only when the person dies.

A lineal descendant TT is a trust established in someone's will for the benefit of their lineal descendants.

A will can establish more than one TT.

A timeline of the administration of an estate and testamentary trust is summarised below.

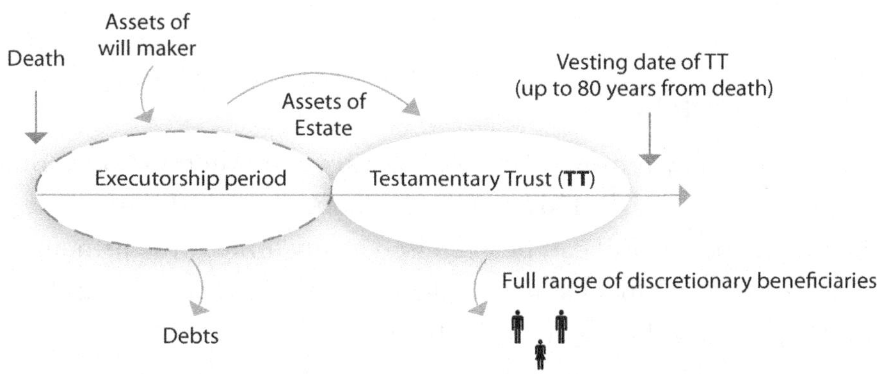

TTs can be used for a variety of purposes – for example to:

a minimise tax – both income tax and capital gains tax
b protect spendthrift beneficiaries from themselves
c care for children
d provide a secure environment for physically or mentally disabled beneficiaries

e keep an inheritance out of the reach of the Family Law Court
f protect an inheritance from a beneficiary's creditors.

Any property can be placed in a TT – including cash, shares (listed and unlisted), residential or commercial property and income-producing assets.

Who controls the assets?

Whoever is named in the will as trustee of the TT controls the trust assets. Like any trust, a TT can be as flexible or as fixed as the testator wishes. The trustee can be given full discretion or no discretion as to who should receive income and capital from the trust and when they should receive it.

The trustee is often the same person who has been appointed as executor of the will, and can also be a beneficiary. For example, a parent can establish a TT for each child's inheritance. Each adult child can be both beneficiary and trustee of their 'own' trust, and may also be an executor of the will.

What is a principal?

The principal may remove or appoint trustees and therefore has ultimate control of the TT. This power of appointment and removal is a discretionary power and can be exercised at any time by the principal. Therefore, the principal has a great deal of control over the TT, as they effectively control the office of the trustee.

The principal may retire and appoint someone else as a replacement. The principal may also appoint a successor and should consider doing so. This means that the power of appointment is flexible, and the current principal is able to nominate who will succeed to the role.

In trusts that are designed to last many years (as is normally the case with TTs) the principal role is the tool by which control of the trust (and in turn the assets) is handed from one generation to the next.

Principal succession

There need not necessarily be a principal provision under a trust deed; however, where there is, a trust deed will normally set out, in some detail, the way in which the role of principal is dealt with on the death or incapacity of the person (or people) originally appointed.

Failing to understand the succession arrangements of a principal can create a range of difficulties, as highlighted in the case of *Montevento Holdings Pty Ltd v Scaffidi (2012) HCA 48*. A full copy of the case is available at http://www.austlii.edu.au/au/cases/cth/HCA/2012/48.html

The case concerned a challenge, by a beneficiary of a discretionary trust, to a change of trustee made by the principal. The challenging beneficiary was Guiseppe Scaffidi who, with Maria (his mother) and Eugenio (his brother), was within the range of potential beneficiaries of the Scaffidi Family Trust.

The original principal of the trust was Antonio Scaffidi (the father). On Antonio's death, Maria became the principal and, by deed Maria, subsequently appointed Eugenio Scaffidi as the principal.

After his appointment, Eugenio appointed Montevento Holdings Pty Ltd (a company of which he was the sole director and shareholder) as the sole trustee, effectively giving him complete control over the trust and its assets.

Guiseppe's challenge to the appointment of the trustee company ultimately failed before the High Court, essentially because the appointment complied with the provisions of the trust deed. The decision highlights the fact that the principal can often gain ultimate control of a trust. It is also a reminder of the importance of regularly reviewing the appropriateness of the principal role in the context of succession planning, particularly where the intention is for multiple beneficiaries to benefit from a discretionary trust over time.

How can a TT be used to minimise tax?

Income received by infant children from a TT is not subject to tax at the usual penalty rates, which can be as high as 66%.

In particular, under section 102AG of the *Income Tax and Assessment Act 1936*, income received from a TT by minors from a deceased estate is assessable at the rates of marginal tax for adults.

This section is not only restricted to children of the deceased, but can be used to advantage adults, even if they are a trustee of the TT.

Example

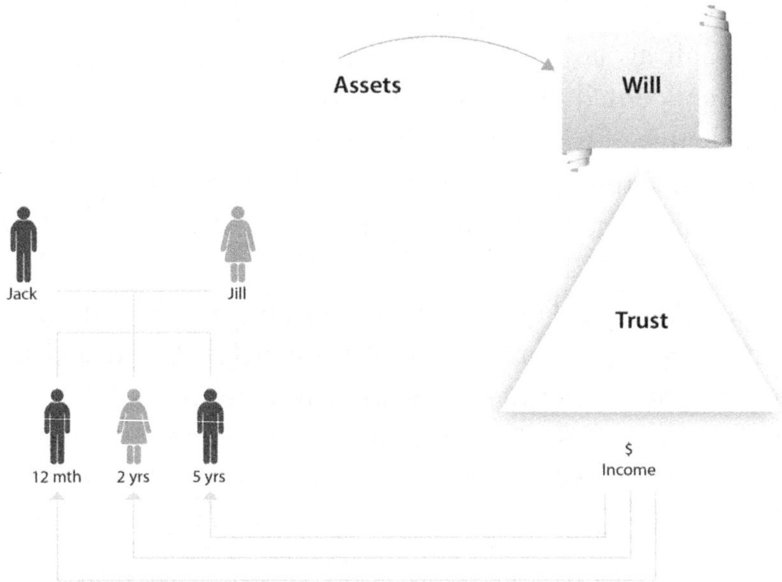

a Jack included a TT in his will.
b When he died, Jill used the trust to distribute income to herself and the children.
c Jill was the trustee.
d She was able to receive, tax-free, a percentage of income each year for herself and the children.

Variations on TT themes

What are 'master trusts'?

Master trusts are commonly used to identify either of the following two situations:

a a 'cascading' TT that seamlessly passes the capital from a single spouse's TT in the first generation to multiple TTs in the second generation (**Figure 1**). This typically resolves many of the potential issues with single TTs in the second generation and third generations without sacrificing flexibility

b a single holding trust, designed to preserve the family wealth, over the course of generations, with a 'custodial' mindset rather than one of ownership (**Figure 2**). Access to the capital and occasionally to the income is carefully managed for the advancement of family members without giving away or dividing the 'family jewels'. This structure has been relatively common within the high and ultra high net worth (**HNW** and **UHNW**) sector for many years, and its use in other segments of the community is increasing, due to changing attitudes to wealth and ease of access to high-level advice.

Cascading TTs

A cascading TT arrangement is a development of the single TT structure that provides further degrees of the flexibility of trust structures. Typical features of a cascading TT are:

a one 'head trust' that will hold the estate of one deceased partner on trust for the surviving spouse

b the surviving partner has full control of income and the timing of the distribution of capital

c a proviso that capital may be distributed only into one or more further TTs, established under the **same will** for the benefit of the next tier of beneficiaries. This might occur on the death of the surviving spouse or earlier at the surviving spouse's option
d normally the second tier of TTs is controlled by the children of the original couple, with their lineal descendants as further potential beneficiaries.

Figure 1 – Cascading TDT

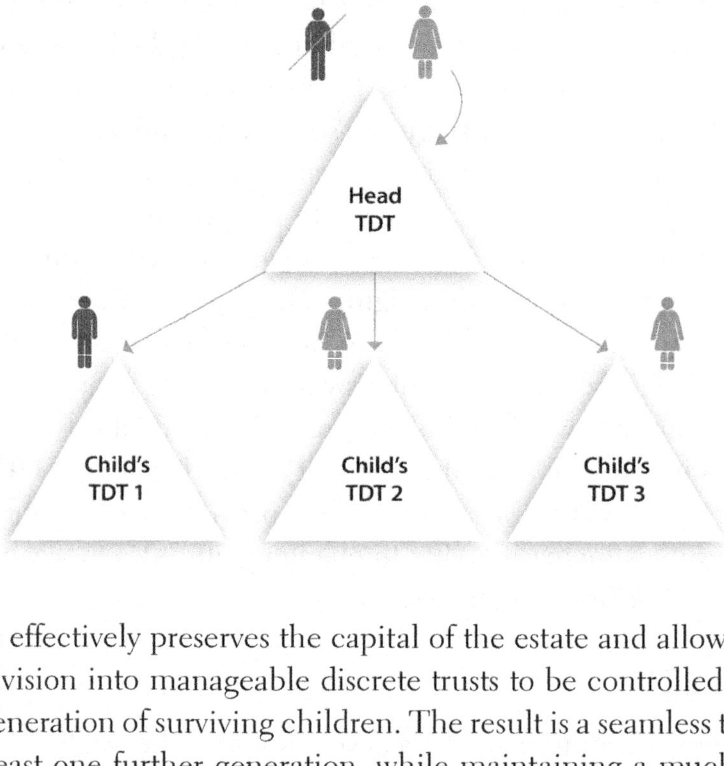

This effectively preserves the capital of the estate and allows a further division into manageable discrete trusts to be controlled by the next generation of surviving children. The result is a seamless transfer to at least one further generation, while maintaining a much more flexible 'life interest' outcome for the surviving spouse.

Master Trusts

Master trusts, sometimes referred to as 'head' or 'dynastic' trusts, are generally distinguished by a structure that selectively makes the proceeds available over time, with limited access to capital. The defining feature of a Master Trust is that each generation is provided with a more custodial role, preserving and increasing the corpus of the original legacy for the benefit of descendants.

Master trusts, and derivations have proved to be a popular method for the holding and preservation of wealth in HNW and UHNW families. Families in this segment often seek to put in place more structured 'custodial' arrangements to maximise the impact and preservation of family wealth over a greater reach of future generations.

As the focus is on being a 'trustee of the family wealth' rather than ownership of wealth within one lifetime, the structure must be carefully considered, and tailored to achieve the wishes of the first testator. Typically there is only one trust created under the will and it has more prescriptive governance, succession and administrative provisions than a usual TT.

Figure 2 – Master trusts

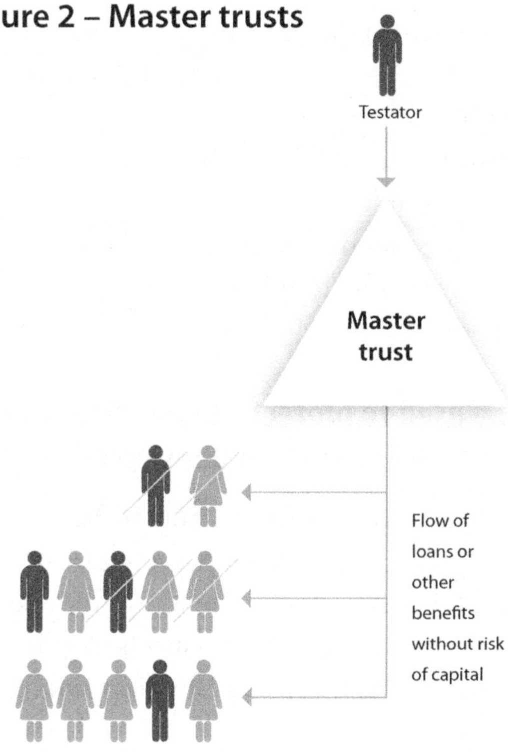

How can a TT help protect an inheritance from a former spouse?

Inheritances, like other assets, can form part of the 'matrimonial property', which is available to the Family Court to distribute in the event of a marriage breakdown and property dispute.

However, if assets are placed in a TT for the beneficiary and their children, then in some circumstances, these assets can be excluded in the division of the matrimonial property. The Family Court, however, may take into account the presence of a TT in determining an equitable distribution of matrimonial assets.

Binding financial agreements are also becoming common practice as a way of ensuring adequate asset protection. This tool is discussed further below.

How can a TT be used to protect an inheritance from a trustee in bankruptcy?

If a beneficiary is having difficulty with creditors, or facing bankruptcy, then any assets that they receive directly under a will could then pass automatically to their creditors.

In these circumstances a TT can help keep assets out of reach of present or future creditors.

The assets (and the income produced by them) held via the TT will still be available for family members and, in particular, the children of the insolvent person.

How can a TT be used to protect a beneficiary from the loss of their social security or pension entitlements?

If a beneficiary is a pensioner, or is likely to be a pensioner and the pension is means tested, then receiving assets directly from a will might disqualify that beneficiary, causing the pension to be reduced.

Under the current means tests, the assets and income of TTs, in some instances, are not assessed as belonging to a person.

The interpretation by governing authorities of legislation relating to pensions, however, depends largely on the officer involved and, in most cases, assets of TTs will be taken into account.

Does a client want their parents, or other persons who are likely to name them as a beneficiary, to give them these benefits in their will?

If a client believes that they might benefit from the advantages of a TT in the distribution of an estate, it might be prudent to discuss the concept with family members – for example, their parents – or any other person who is likely to name them as a beneficiary in their will.

Letter of wishes

A LETTER OF WISHES is intended to provide general guidance to the executor or trustee of a person's estate following their death. While the document is not legally binding, it can have strong moral sway.

A letter of wishes is a very personal document and can deal with a range of issues including:

a wishes in relation to assets which the will-maker may have effectively controlled during their lifetime, but will not form part of their estate – for example, assets in discretionary trusts, SMSFs or offshore entities
b the names of advisers or family friends from whom assistance should be obtained in relation to financial planning, accounting services, legal advice, insurance brokerage, stockbroking, religious guidance or other matters
c personal assets, particularly those with emotional value, such as jewellery, items of collection, other personal effects or family heirlooms
d any charities or causes that the will-maker would like the beneficiaries to consider
e the location of important documents such as deeds, title records and financial information;
f any wishes or directions as to how infant children should be cared for
g directions in relation to funeral arrangements and burial
h any other matters that the will-maker would like their executors or trustees to take into account.

Enduring Power of Attorney

AN ENDURING POWER of attorney is a document empowering a person (or persons) to act on behalf of another with respect to the giver's proprietary rights. These include anything to do with the giver's property, assets or rights with respect to property.

Powers of attorney can be either general or limited. Under a general power of attorney, the attorney is able to do virtually everything the person giving the power could legally do. Under a limited power of attorney, the power is restricted in some way. For example, the attorney may be appointed only for a certain time or only to perform certain acts.

A power of attorney should be given only to someone the client trusts completely. It is an extremely useful document, in the right hands, but very dangerous in the wrong hands.

Witnessing power of attorneys

In each Australian state, legal practitioners are authorised witnesses for most forms of powers of attorney.

Documents that are directly related to medical issues, however, can normally only be witnessed by a medical practitioner.

In some states, financial-related power of attorney documents can be witnessed by a range of authorised signatories.

While there are numerous inconsistencies between the various states, each state does at least set out in some detail the witnessing requirement for each document as part of the standard government form.

Is an enduring power of attorney necessary?

An enduring power of attorney should always be used in an estate planning exercise. Enduring powers of attorney remain valid even if the donor loses capacity, in contrast with other types of attorney documents, which become void under those circumstances.

If clients lose mental capacity, someone must be appointed to look after their affairs. If they have granted an enduring power of attorney, they will have made the choice of that person (or persons) themselves.

If a client does not grant an enduring power of attorney, someone (their spouse, children, trusted relative or friend) will need to apply to a court or a government tribunal to be appointed. It is likely that an officer from the government will also become involved in the management of their affairs, which generally adds significant extra (and unnecessary) expense, both financially and emotionally.

Advanced Health Directives

An issue that comes up relatively regularly in estate planning exercises is that of Advanced Health Directives (**AHD**).

In most jurisdictions, an AHD is essentially a document, addressed to a person's medical practitioner, which sets out the level of care that the person would like to receive in a series of specific situations.

The document is usually crafted as a 'multiple choice' questionnaire, listing dozens of typical medical scenarios, and completed in consultation with a client's GP.

As the document is a medical, not a legal, one, most lawyers simply provide access to the standard document rather than provide advice on it.

One important issue to note is that in no Australian state does an AHD allow for euthanasia style directions to be articulated.

A person who has legal capacity may revoke their AHD at any time.

There are several significant practical difficulties with AHDs and, in summary, the main related issues are:

a the person making the AHD wants to have a 'turn off the switch' provision (or perhaps even the option of euthanasia). No AHD allows this. Unless the donor has specific religious or personal objectives, many of the questions are somewhat irrelevant

b the attitude of a donor at the time of signing the AHD is not necessarily an indication of what their attitude might be, at some future time, when the issue arises. Anecdotally many doctors are unwilling to rely on a document drawn up years earlier;

c the document must be completed in consultation with a GP but, as it is unlikely that the same GP would be involved in any sort of emergency situation, the doctor actually performing the medical treatment, for instance, would be unlikely to try to find the AHD or rely on it if it were found

d in contrast, doctors will generally give significant weight to whoever is appointed as the enduring power of attorney. If that enduring power of attorney is also a next of kin and if there is no hint of any dispute in the immediate family group, then the wishes of the person seeking medical treatment will generally be respected.

Binding financial agreements

THE *FAMILY LAW Act 1975 (Cth)* allows parties in a relationship to enter into a binding financial agreement (**BFA**) to provide for the manner in which matrimonial assets (including those assets brought to the relationship by the parties) are to be divided in the event of separation. A BFA can be drafted to take account of specific assets in existence at the time the agreement is made and/or those acquired subsequent to the agreement.

While a BFA might not always be completely 'water tight' if subsequently disputed, it generally provides the parties with a level of certainty in relation to the distribution of assets resulting from a relationship breakdown. A BFA should be binding on the parties to the agreement if:

a the agreement is signed by both parties
b before signing the agreements, each party was provided with independent legal advice as to:
 (i) the effect of the agreement on their rights
 (ii) the advantages and disadvantages of entering into the BFA
c each spouse is provided with a signed statement stating that the advice was provided
d after the agreement is signed, the original agreement is given to one of the parties and a copy given to the other (or their legal representatives)
e the agreement has not been terminated or set aside by a Court.

There must also be full disclosure of the property and resources of each spouse as at the date of commencement of cohabitation and at present. For example:

a **real property** – the address, title particulars (if known) and estimated value of the property as at date of commencement of cohabitation and at present
b **mortgages** – full name of the mortgagee, the title reference to the mortgage (if known) and any particular terms of the mortgage that might assist in relation to understanding the mortgage
c **loans** – full particulars of the loan and any particular terms relating to it
d **companies** – details including company names, names of directors and the company's shareholdings
e **savings/investments** – details including the name of the investment and relevant institution, the number of units or shares (if relevant) and the estimated current value of each savings/investment as at date of commencement of cohabitation and at present
f **superannuation and interests in a trust, an estate, or an entitlement to a personal injuries verdict** – full details, including the name of the superannuation fund and relevant entitlements, details of the trust deed and names of the relevant beneficiaries.

Having listed all the assets, liabilities and resources of each spouse, the following details are required as to how that property is to be dealt with on a breakdown of the relationship:

a details (if relevant) of the existence of any unresolved matrimonial property and/or maintenance issues between a spouse and an estranged former spouse
b whether the agreement is to be enforceable in the event of the death of a spouse
c whether there is to be a sharing of expenses and/or the payment of monies by one party to another
d what will amount to a cessation of the relationship.

Unless there is an intention to leave some assets of a spouse outside the operation of the BFA, every asset of the parties should be disclosed and ultimately dealt with in the agreement.

The most substantial benefit to the parties from entering into a compliant BFA is that the Family Court cannot make an order that is inconsistent with the terms of the agreement.

However, the Family Court may set aside a BFA if the court is satisfied that:

a the agreement was obtained by fraud (including non-disclosure of a material matter)

b the agreement is void, voidable or unenforceable in the circumstances that have arisen since the agreement was made

c it is impracticable for the agreement or a part of the agreement to be carried out

d since the making of the agreement, a material change in circumstances has occurred (being circumstances relating to the care, welfare and development of a child of the marriage) and, as a result of the change, a party to the agreement will suffer hardship if the Court does not set the agreement aside

e in respect of the making of a BFA, a party to the agreement engaged in conduct that was, in all the circumstances, unconscionable.

It is a fundamental feature of a valid BFA that each party make full disclosure of all personal details, property and resources to ensure that any decision about how the property and resources are to be divided in the event of a relationship breakdown is made with full consent and understanding by both parties.

Whilst the subject of entering into a BFA can be a difficult topic, a BFA can provide a level of certainty as to how assets are to be divided in the event of a relationship breakdown.

Relationships

What is a spouse?

The question as to what kind of relationship satisfies the definition of a 'spouse' comes up regularly.

The Tax Act sets out one of the most commonly used definitions.

A '*spouse*' of an individual includes:

a another individual (whether of the same sex or a different sex) with whom the individual is in a relationship that is registered, under a State law or Territory law prescribed for the purposes of section 22B of the *Acts Interpretation Act 1901*, as a kind of relationship prescribed for the purposes of that section
b another individual who, although not legally married to the individual, lives with the individual, on a genuine domestic basis, in a relationship as a couple.

What is a de facto?

A person will be in a *de facto* relationship with another person, if:

a the persons are not legally married to each other
b the persons are not related by family (see subsection (6)) and
c having regard to all the circumstances of their relationship, they have a relationship as a couple living together on a genuine domestic basis.

Some specific circumstances, which are taken into account by the courts to determine whether a relationship does amount to a *de facto* relationship, include any or all of the following:

a the duration of the relationship
b the nature and extent of their common residence

c whether a sexual relationship exists
d the degree of financial dependence or interdependence, and any arrangements for financial support, between them
e the ownership, use and acquisition of their property
f the degree of mutual commitment to a shared life
g whether the relationship is or was registered under a prescribed law of a State or Territory as a prescribed kind of relationship
h the care and support of children
i the reputation and public aspects of the relationship.

Whether a relationship is sufficient to satisfy the *de facto* definition is not clear.

One family law decision, for example, involved a situation where a woman argued that she and the man involved 'spent time together at various times in various places, had a sexual relationship, and expressed love and affection for each other' for more than 17 years. The argument was that this was a '*de facto* relationship' within the meaning of s4AA of the Family Law Act.

The man denied 'any such relationship' and instead claimed it was simply 'an affair' and the woman was a 'kept woman'. Both parties agreed that they had travelled overseas together and the man had paid the woman $24,000 to help her buy a home and $2,000 monthly, increasing progressively to $3,000 a month.

While the court rejected the man's argument that 'exclusivity' was necessary for a *de facto* relationship to exist, the facts here did not support the woman's argument that they were *de factos*.

The quotation that best captures the decision of the Court is as follows:

'the key to that definition (i.e. de facto) is the manifestation of a relationship where both the parties have so merged their lives that they were, for all practical purposes 'living together' as a couple on a genuine domestic basis. It is the manifesta-

tion of 'coupledom' which involves the merger of two lives as just described, that is the core of a de facto relationship as defined and to which each of the statutory factors (and others that want to apply to a particular relationship) are directed'.

'Interdependency' relationships

Two persons (whether or not related by family) have an interdependency relationship under this section if:

- a they have a close personal relationship
- b they live together
- c one or each of them provides the other with financial support
- d one or each of them provides the other with domestic support and personal care.

In addition, two persons (whether or not related by family) also have an interdependency relationship under this section if:

- a they have a close personal relationship
- b they do not satisfy one or more of the requirements of an interdependency relationship mentioned in paragraphs (1)(b), (c) and (d)
- c the reason they do not satisfy those requirements is that either or both of them suffer from a physical, intellectual or psychiatric disability.

The superannuation legislation (under regulation 1.04AAAA) sets out a number of tests in relation to whether a relationship between two people amounts to an interdependency relationship.

In summary, the tests include:

- a the duration of the relationship
- b whether or not a sexual relationship exists
- c the ownership, use and acquisition of property

d the degree of mutual commitment to a shared life
e the care and support of children
f the reputation and public aspects of the relationship
g the degree of emotional support
h the extent to which the relationship is one of mere convenience
i any evidence suggesting that the parties intend the relationship to be permanent.

Chapter 2

JOINT TENANCY V TENANCY IN COMMON

Joint Tenancies

There are two ways property can be owned 'jointly' – namely, via a joint tenancy or a tenancy in common.

What is a Joint Tenancy?

A joint tenancy is where two or more persons own the same property together. Together, the joint tenants own the whole asset, sharing undivided ownership.

Common examples include real estate, shares and bank accounts. Many couples, for example, will both own the family home and have a joint bank account.

It is not possible to hold property as joint tenants in unequal shares.

What happens on death?

In a joint tenancy, the principle of survivorship applies. Under this principle, the surviving joint tenant automatically acquires the ownership of the deceased joint tenant's share, regardless of what a will may state.

In other words, the survivorship principle applies even if a person's will tries to dispose of a joint asset; the surviving joint tenant automatically inherits.

Tenancy in common

What is a tenancy in common?

A tenancy in common occurs where two or more persons discretely own their own share of the asset.

Both, or all tenants are able to sell or otherwise dispose of their share in the asset.

The ownership does not need to be equal, for example, one tenant may own 60% and the other may own 40%.

None of the tenants in common is entitled to exclusive possession of any part of the asset, without the other.

What happens on death?

If one owner dies, the other does not automatically become the new owner.

A person's will regulates where their share of the asset goes.

What determines whether an asset is held jointly or as tenants in common?

There are numerous principles that determine whether individuals own property as joint tenants or as tenants in common.

Generally, the law presumes that co-owners of property hold that property as joint tenants.

For example, where a certificate of title, a share certificate or a bank account is in the names of two life spouses, then they will hold the property as joint tenants.

However, it is necessary to look at the intention of the parties when they acquired the property in question. Did they intend to hold it as joint tenants? Or did they intend to hold it as tenants in common?

Severing a joint tenancy

Reasons why it may be important to sever

If an asset is held in a joint tenancy, then that arrangement can be severed and converted to tenancy in common.

Following conversion, the owner can then unilaterally dispose of their share of the property during their lifetime or via their will on death.

Example 1

Ron and his sister, Sue, bought a small investment property together as joint tenants before either of them was married. After his marriage, Ron wished to change the arrangement to a tenancy in common so that his interest could pass to his new wife rather than automatically to his sister.

Example 2

Ron and Judy purchased their family home as joint tenants. A few years later, Judy established a business and was concerned about losing everything if the business failed. If Ron were to die, Judy did not want the house to be owned 100% in her name. She preferred that Ron's interest, at least, be owned via a TT. In this case, Judy and Ron should sever the joint tenancy arrangement and convert their ownership to tenants in common so that Ron can at least deal with his interest in the property under his will.

How can a joint tenancy be severed?

In the case of personal property (such as shares or bank accounts) it might be enough for the parties to sign a written declaration, stating that it was their intention, at the time of purchase, to hold the purchased property as tenants in common.

An alternative is for the parties subsequently to agree in writing that they hold the property as tenants in common.

In the case of land, a person can sell their interest in a joint property to a third party who then holds that interest as a tenant in common.

Joint owners may also sever a joint tenancy by agreement. That is, they can simply agree that from a certain point in time they will hold the property as tenants in common.

Capital Gains Tax and Stamp Duty

Stamp duty

Most states provide a full exemption from stamp duty for a change in the manner of holding (for example, a change from joint tenancy to tenancy in common) on the basis that the value of the interests at the time does not change.

Capital Gains Tax

Section 108-7 of the *ITAA 1997* treats a CGT asset that is owned jointly as if that interest were held as tenants in common. In other words, each individual who owns a CGT asset jointly is notionally treated as owning a separate asset constituted by an equal interest in the asset.

Provided that there is no change in the beneficial ownership, then the conversion of a joint tenancy to tenancy in common, or vice versa, has no CGT consequences.

Chapter 3

SUPERANNUATION

What happens to superannuation upon death?

A person's superannuation might not form part of their estate and is often dealt with at the discretion of the super fund's trustee, depending upon the fund's trust deed.

Who are eligible recipients of superannuation benefits on death?

A superannuation fund trustee may only pay a superannuation death benefit to a deceased member's 'dependant', or their 'legal personal representative'.

A member wanting to provide for part of their superannuation benefit to go to a non-dependant can do so via their will. For example, a member wanting to have their sibling benefit from their superannuation entitlements would do so by providing for the member's death benefit to be paid to their estate, and then providing in their will for payment of that benefit to the sibling.

Who is a 'dependant'?

The term 'dependant' has its ordinary meaning of someone who was receiving and relying on financial support from the deceased at the time of their death. Superannuation legislation extends the term 'dependant' to include any of the following, even if they were not receiving financial support from the deceased:

a the deceased's spouse – including a legal spouse, *de facto* at the time of death and a same sex partner
b a child of the deceased – including a natural child, an adopted child, a stepchild (while his or her natural parent is alive) and an ex-nuptial child. The child can be any age

c any person with whom the deceased had an 'interdependency relationship' at the time of their death as explained in Chapter 1.

Who is the deceased's legal personal representative?

The executor appointed by the deceased's will is the legal personal representative. If there is no will or no one is validly appointed by the will, the person who applies to the Court and is granted the right to administer the estate is the deceased's legal personal representative.

If a superannuation death benefit is paid to the legal personal representative, it will form part of the deceased's estate and be distributed along with the other assets according to the terms of the will (if there is one) or the intestacy rules (if there is not).

The role of the trustee

In administering a superannuation fund, a trustee is normally given a number of discretionary powers.

It is generally up to the trustee of the relevant fund to determine whether a person's superannuation benefits are paid to a dependant directly or to their estate. The trustee of the fund may pay the superannuation benefits directly to a person's dependants, and thus bypass the estate.

It is also possible for the moneys to pass through the estate and be dealt with by the will and, for example, form part of a TT.

The trustee may also have the discretion to determine how those benefits will be paid – either by lump sum or income stream, or possibly a combination of both (although if a benefit is to be paid from a superannuation fund to the estate it can only be paid in the form of a lump sum).

Income stream

A superannuation death benefit may only be paid as an income stream to a dependant of the deceased member. Special transitional rules apply to death benefit income streams commenced prior to 1 July 2007.

If an income stream superannuation death benefit is paid to a child, then the income stream must be converted to a lump sum superannuation death benefit once the child reaches the age of 25. The decision to pay an income stream to a child needs to take this into account, especially if there is likely to be a large lump sum passing to the child at age 25.

Where a member has reached preservation age, and is already receiving their superannuation benefit as an income stream, it is possible to nominate a reversionary beneficiary for their benefit to ensure that, upon the member's death, the income stream is paid to their nominated beneficiary.

The tax treatment of both lump sum and income stream superannuation death benefits depends upon a number of factors and will be considered in detail later on.

Ultimately, the trust deed governing a superannuation fund (together with any valid nominations) will determine the process for dealing with a person's superannuation assets upon their death.

Typical employer funds

Most employer funds leave the ultimate discretion to the trustees of the fund.

They usually allow the member to nominate whom they would like to receive the funds after their death, and this nomination is usually followed.

Retail funds

Many retail funds leave the decisions to the trustee of the fund.

Where the trust deed allows a member to nominate (on a non-binding basis) a beneficiary, that nomination will invariably be followed unless there are compelling reasons against doing so.

Many retail funds also permit binding nominations, which, if valid, must be followed by the trustee (see below).

Withdrawal of funds prior to death

When a member is over 60 years of age, generally all super benefits will be tax-free on withdrawal.

The payment of a lump sum to the member before death, which they hold and will become part of their estate upon death, will avoid any tax on super benefits that would be payable if the amount was left in the superannuation environment and distributed to a non-dependant (i.e. adult children) after death.

Where a member withdraws their super benefits as a lump sum, any earnings and capital gains on the investments will occur outside the super environment and will not be concessionally taxed – that is, they will be taxed at the marginal rates of tax. Where clients leave their super benefits in the superannuation environment and continue with pensions, any earnings, capital gains and pension payments will be tax-free.

Some commentators argue that it is possible to 'pre-sign' a super benefits withdrawal form to enable it to be dated by someone after the member's death (the date would be some time before death). More practically and ignoring the question of fraud, the Australian Taxation Office (**ATO**) requires physical withdrawal in order to avoid the imposition of tax and therefore 'pre-signing' will be ineffective.

SMSFs

What is a self managed super fund?

An SMSF performs the same role as other types of superannuation funds, by investing contributions and making them available to members on retirement. The main difference is that the members of a SMSF are also the trustees of the fund; they control the investment of their contributions and the payment of their benefits. As all members are trustees, they are in a position to ensure that their interests as members are protected.

Generally, a superannuation fund is an SMSF if, with a few exceptions:

a it has a trust deed that meets the requirements of the *Superannuation Industry (Supervision) Act 1993* (**SIS**)
b it has fewer than five members
c each member of the fund is a trustee
d no member of the fund is an employee of another member of the fund, unless they are related
e no trustee of the fund receives any remuneration for their services as trustee.

How is a SMSF established?

There are several steps that need to be undertaken to set up an SMSF. These include:

a obtaining a trust deed and ensuring that it is correctly drafted to achieve the fund's objectives
b appointing trustees to manage the fund. To be an SMSF, all members must be appointed as trustees of the fund or directors of a corporate trustee

c. electing to become a regulated fund. Elections must be lodged with the ATO, and entitle the fund to receive concessional taxation treatment
d. obtaining a TFN and Australian Business Number (**ABN**).

In most cases, the continuing trustee of a SMSF will decide how a deceased member's death benefit will be treated, unless a binding nomination has been made.

Therefore, it is important to ensure that a person is comfortable with the choice of person(s) who will continue as trustee of their fund after their death.

Who can be a trustee?

Anyone over the age of 18 can be a trustee of a superannuation fund unless they are a 'disqualified person' under the SIS. A person is a `disqualified person' if:

a. the person has been convicted of an offence involving dishonesty
b. the person has been subject to a civil penalty order under the SIS
c. the person is an insolvent under administration.

Special rules apply in relation to the trusteeship of sole member funds. It is not possible for an SMSF to have only one member and one individual trustee, as there is no separation of the legal and beneficial ownership. Therefore, to establish an SMSF with a sole member, a co-trustee or corporate trustee must be appointed. The co-trustee should be a relative of the sole member.

An SMSF may have a company as trustee, provided that:

a. if there are two or more members, every member of the fund is a director of the corporate trustee, and every director of the corporate trustee is a member of the fund
b. if there is only one member, that member is the sole director of the corporate trustee or one of only two directors and the other

director is either a relative, or a person who is not a relative and not an employee of the member.

Disqualification provisions similar to those outlined above apply to directors of corporate trustees.

What's involved in being a trustee?

Trustees need to familiarize themselves with the legislative requirements and administrative responsibilities of running an SMSF. Failure to do so might jeopardize the fund's eligibility for tax concessions or result in penalties being imposed on the trustees.

The administrative obligations imposed on trustees are wide ranging and include:

a preparing and keeping accurate accounting records and annual returns
b lodging a combined income tax and regulatory return with the ATO each year
c reporting member contribution information to the ATO
d reporting payments of benefits (superannuation pensions, annuities and eligible termination payments) made to members
e paying an annual supervisory levy to the ATO upon lodgement of their combined annual return
f arranging for the financial accounts and statements of the fund to be audited each year by an approved auditor.

What restrictions apply?

SMSFs are regulated by the ATO, which is responsible for enforcing the restrictions contained in SIS. These restrictions include:

a an SMSF must be maintained for the sole purpose of providing benefits to members upon their retirement, or to their dependants (as defined under SIS) if the member dies before retirement

b trustees must not lend money, or provide direct or indirect financial assistance from the fund, to a member or a member's relative
c SMSFs are prohibited from borrowing money except in certain limited circumstances
d trustees are prohibited from acquiring assets from a 'related party' of the superannuation fund, which includes all members of the fund together with their relatives, partners and any companies or trusts that they control. The limited exceptions to this rule include assets acquired at market value if:
    (i) the asset is a listed security (for example, shares, units or bonds listed on an approved Stock Exchange)
    (ii) the asset is 'business real property' (again, as defined under SIS).
e trustees must keep superannuation assets separate from their personal assets and the assets held by employers who contribute to the fund
f investments must be on an arm's length basis.

What is an investment strategy?

The trustees of every SMSF are required to prepare and implement an investment strategy for the fund. Although SIS does not set out details of what the strategy should contain, it states that the strategy must reflect the purpose and circumstances of the fund and have particular regard to:

a investing in such a way as to maximise member returns, taking into account the risk associated in holding the investment
b appropriate diversification and the benefits of investing across a number of asset classes (for example, shares, property, fixed deposit) in a long-term investment strategy
c the ability of the superannuation fund to pay benefits as well as other costs of the superannuation fund as they become due and payable.

The strategy should set out the investment objectives of the fund and the methods that the fund will employ to achieve these objectives.

Who can receive a death benefit?

A superannuation fund trustee can only pay a superannuation death benefit to a dependant, or to the deceased's legal personal representative.

Taxation of superannuation benefits

If the recipient of the death benefit receives the benefit as an income stream, it will be treated as a member benefit instead of a death benefit, if the benefit is paid after the latest of:

a six months after the death
b three months after the grant of probate
c if the payment is delayed due to legal action relating to the benefit, six months after the legal action ceases
d if there are reasonable delays, six months after processing is completed
e if the Commissioner has not made a decision. This decision can affect whether the benefit is treated as a member benefit or death benefit.

Who qualifies as a dependant for tax purposes?

The definition of a dependant for tax purposes is different from the definition under the *Superannuation Industry (Supervision) Act* 1993.

A dependant for tax purposes is:

a the legal spouse or de facto at the time of death
b a former legal spouse or former de facto
c a natural, adopted, step or ex-nuptial child less than 18 years old
d any person financially dependent on the deceased at the time of death.

Payment to death benefit dependants

If the dependency test is satisfied, taxation will depend on whether the benefit is a lump sum or income stream. In the case of a lump sum, the benefit will be tax-free.

A death benefit paid in the form of an income stream to a dependent child of the deceased member (a child under the age of 25 years) will also be tax-free until they attain the age of 25, at which time (or earlier) the child must cash the benefit as a lump sum.

If the benefit is an income stream, taxation will depend on whether the benefit is paid from an element that is taxed or not taxed in the fund. If the element is taxed in the fund, the benefit will be tax-free, if the dependant is at least 60 years old or if the deceased was at least 60 years old.

Where the element is untaxed in the fund, if either the dependant or deceased was aged 60 or above, they will be entitled to a 10% offset. If neither was aged 60, the untaxed amount is included in the dependant's assessable income and taxed at usual rates, and the recipient is entitled to a 15% offset.

Payments to non-dependants

Since the changes to the superannuation regime in July 2007, non-dependants and children over the age of 25 (other than children with a permanent disability) may only receive superannuation death benefits as a lump sum, and not as an income stream. However, non-dependants and children who began receiving an income stream prior to the changes will be taxed in the same way as are income streams to dependants above.

Superannuation death benefits paid as a lump sum to non-dependants are taxed in the following manner:

- a the tax-free component of the death benefit is tax-free
- b the taxable component is taxed at:
  - (i) a maximum of 15% – for the taxed element
  - (ii) a maximum of 30% – for the untaxed element

These maximum rates are achieved by the death benefit recipient including all amounts of the taxed element in their assessable income for that year and receiving a tax offset on those amounts.

'Death Tax'

Historically, the ATO sought to argue that a pension (and the tax exemption thereon) ceased as soon as the member in receipt of the pension died. The exception to this position was where a dependent beneficiary of the deceased was automatically entitled under the super fund's deed, or rules of the pension, to receive the pension on the death of the member. This type of pension is often referred to as an auto reversionary pension (**ARP**).

The Federal Government, however, announced that, with effect from 1 July 2012, a tax exemption applies following the death of a SMSF member in receipt of a pension until that pension has been paid out of the fund. The main requirement for the exemption to apply is that the pension is paid out of the fund as soon as practicable.

As a result, an ARP is not required to ensure access to the tax exemption.

Death benefit paid to deceased's legal personal representative

If a death benefit is paid to the legal personal representative, it will become part of the deceased's estate and be distributed in accordance with the rest of the will or, if there is no will, in accordance with the intestacy rules. In these circumstances, there is no prohibition on who can receive the payment.

Where a superannuation death benefit is paid to a deceased's estate, taxation of the benefit depends upon who is ultimately entitled to receive the funds under the will. Where the trustee has a discretion to pay the funds either to dependants or non-dependants (for example, under a TT), it is assumed that non-dependants will receive the benefit. Any tax is imposed on the trustees of the estate.

Is a trustee bound by a death benefit nomination?

There are two types of nomination that the trustee may receive in relation to paying a death benefit:

a non-binding nominations
b binding nominations.

Non-binding nominations

When a person makes a non-binding nomination, they are informing the trustee of the fund as to the persons to whom they wish their superannuation benefits to be paid.

The trustee is not legally bound to comply with a non-binding death benefit nomination, although the trustee is legally required to take it into account when deciding to whom the superannuation benefits are to be paid upon death.

Binding nominations

If the trust fund allows it, a person may make a binding nomination.

A binding nomination is a written election, made by the member, which directs the trustee of the fund to pay benefits to any dependants, or to their legal personal representatives.

The trustee is legally bound to comply with a valid binding nomination.

In SMSFs, it is possible to 'hard wire' binding nominations into the deed for the fund.

Superannuation death benefits

In virtually every estate planning exercise, the issue of how members of a super fund can direct payment of benefits, on death, invariably arises.

Essentially a member of a superannuation fund has three main choices for specifying what should happen in relation to their superannuation entitlements on death (assuming the proposed recipient is entitled at law), namely:

a nomination – the trustee is bound to deal with a member's benefit in their best interests. Before making a decision, the trustee will normally make enquiries as to the member's family situation, who their dependants are, the provisions of their will and other relevant circumstances
b a non-binding nomination – the trustee is not bound by a non-binding notice and has an absolute discretion as to where the death benefit will be paid. Where a non-binding notice is made, it should be taken into account as part of any decision by the trustee as to how to distribute the benefit
c a binding nomination – the trustee is obliged to distribute a member's death benefits in accordance with a valid binding notice.

Binding nominations have the potential to allow members to protect their death benefits from disputes; where there is no nomination or a non-binding one, a trustee's decision can be challenged. Binding nominations can also be used as part of a member's overall estate plan – for example, as part of a tax planning strategy for infant children or as an asset protection strategy for adult children.

Where there is a valid BDBN, the trustee has no discretion to pay death benefits other than in accordance with the notice.

The following are critical points to note, in this area:

a if a member's circumstances change and they have failed to update their BDBN, it will, subject in some situations to automatic lapsing (for example, every three years), continue to be binding on the trustee
b the trust deed for the superannuation fund must allow for a BDBN to be given to the trustee of the fund – even some recently set up deeds do not always have such a provision
c unless specifically provided for in the deed, a BDBN will often need to be 'refreshed' every three years. An alternative approach is to update the trust deed for the fund to 'hardwire' the nomination into the deed, avoiding the need to refresh the nomination regularly.

Specific requirements of binding nominations

As with many other aspects of estate planning, whenever considering a BDBN, the starting point should always be the requirements set out under the trust deed. Indeed, a BDBN can only be used where the deed allows one to be made.

Below are examples of some of the requirements that are generally set out in trust deeds before a nomination will be held to be binding; the first three are expressly required by legislation:

a must be in writing
b must be signed, and dated, by the Member in the presence of two witnesses, each of whom has turned 18 and neither of whom is a person mentioned in the notice
c must contain a declaration signed and dated by the witnesses stating that the notice was signed by the Member in their presence
d will not lapse by the passing of time
e may be revoked by the Member by written notice to the Trustee at any time
f must contain sufficient details to identify the Member
g must contain sufficient details to identify one or more Beneficiaries for each category of benefits selected.

While almost all trust deeds that allow BDBNs will have provisions along the lines outlined above, at times there will be additional provisions that are not necessarily expected. Some examples are:

a a requirement that the trust deed for the superannuation fund cannot be amended in a way that has an impact on any BDBN without the consent of each member who has made one
b a provision that empowers the trustee to accept amended BDBNs from the financial attorney of a member
c the trustee may be required to consider and accept a BDBN before it is valid

d there may be a requirement that a particular table or form, which sets out the percentage entitlement of each beneficiary, be embedded into the BDBN.

When should binding nominations be used?

Broadly, a binding nomination will be useful in the following circumstances:

a people in second or third marriages;
b where there are children from different relationships
c where there are concerns about beneficiaries challenging the estate.

The main advantage of making a binding nomination is the certainty it provides.

By completing a binding nomination the risk of challenges to the fund that might arise on the member's death are minimised.

The main disadvantage of making a binding nomination is that the nomination locks the trustee of the fund into directing any death benefits to the dependants or to the estate nominated. If a person's circumstances change, for instance, due to divorce, separation or bankruptcy, the certainty that was hoped for might be negated.

Superannuation entitlements – case law

Superannuation entitlements are often seen as the most significant assets in any estate planning exercise.

Critically, however, superannuation benefits need to be regulated in a way that complements a wider estate planning exercise.

Arguably, the leading case in relation to superannuation death benefit planning is *Katz v Grossman [2005] NSWSC 934*.

The case involved Katz bringing an action against his sister, Grossman, and her husband, claiming an interest in their father's self managed superannuation fund (**SMSF**).

In particular:

a. the father and mother were, originally, the individual trustees of an SMSF
b. the mother died some years before the father and, at that time, Grossman was appointed as a co-trustee in order to ensure that the SMSF continued to comply with the relevant superannuation legislation
c. when the father died, Grossman appointed her husband as a co-trustee
d. the father had made a non-binding nomination, indicating that he wanted his superannuation entitlements divided equally between Katz and Grossman
e. Grossman and her husband ignored the nomination and paid the entire benefit to her.

On the basis that all trustees had been validly appointed at the relevant times, the challenge by Katz was, obviously, that if the father had utilised a binding death benefit nomination, there would likely not have been any successful challenge to the ultimate payment.

Some of the other planning strategies that can be used to regulate the distribution of superannuation benefits on death are:

a. including automatic adjustment clauses under the terms of a will, to take into account benefits that are received directly from a superannuation fund
b. mandating the succession of trusteeship of superannuation fund
c. entrenching approval mechanisms for death benefit payments – for example, by prohibiting a payment until the trustee receives consent from a trusted third party.

The case of *Ioppolo & Hesford v Conti & Anor [2013]* WASC 389 provides another example of how unintended consequences can arise where the control of an SMSF is not carefully considered as part of a comprehensive estate plan.

In this case:

a. the husband and wife originally established an SMSF and were the individual trustees
b. following the wife's death, the husband appointed a corporate trustee, of which he was the sole director and shareholder, in order to comply with the relevant superannuation legislation
c. the corporate trustee (with the husband as sole director), then resolved to pay the entirety of the wife's superannuation entitlements to the husband, not to her legal personal representative, for distribution pursuant to her will
d. the executors of the will sought to unwind the distribution, partly because of a direction in the will that related to the superannuation entitlements
e. in particular, the executors argued that the husband failed to act in a *bona fide* manner because of the provision in the will
f. in dismissing the executor's claim and allowing the husband to retain all of the wife's superannuation benefits, the court confirmed that there is no obligation under the superannuation legislation for a surviving trustee automatically to appoint the executors of a former co trustee as replacement trustees of an SMSF.

In many ways, the decision simply reinforced the principle from the *Katz v Grossman* case some years earlier.

Refreshing of cost base

AFTER DEATH, IN addition to any taxes triggered on the payment of funds or distribution of assets to dependants, the SMSF itself also must pay tax, at a rate of 10%, on the difference between the cost base and market value of each asset the subject of payment at the date of death.

As any sale of a capital asset prior to death (assuming the SMSF continues in pension mode) is tax-free, one strategy often adopted is to actively 'refresh' the cost base of the assets in the SMSF. This is achieved by the following steps:

a assets with large capital gains are regularly sold and then reacquired, or other assets are acquired
b the sale and reacquisition ensure that the cost base of the asset, for the SMSF, is regularly uplifted
c on death, the likely capital gain in relation to any particular asset is therefore minimised.

This approach needs to be managed carefully to ensure the anti-avoidance provisions of the Tax Act are not enlivened. This point is discussed in more detail below.

Trustees of SMSF

The death of a trustee (or director of a corporate trustee) of an SMSF can cause complications if the implications are not carefully considered.

Corporate trustees

If the will-maker is a shareholder in the corporate trustee of an SMSF, it is important to specify the recipient of those shares in their will.

The Corporations Act gives shareholders voting rights and allows them to vote out directors of the company (subject to any provision to the contrary in the constitution of the corporate trustee).

Shareholders thus hold a considerable amount of power and care must be taken to ensure that appropriate beneficiaries of the shares are chosen and included in the will.

The beneficiaries holding the shares will often have the responsibility of appointing a new director of the trustee company of the SMSF.

The new director would, in turn, along with any other directors of the company, exercise discretion in paying death benefits, unless a binding nomination has been made.

Corporate trustees and SMSFs

While the initial setup costs of a corporate trustee are generally higher than for individuals, there is a range of reasons why the use of a company is beneficial, including:

a. the use of a corporate trustee provides limited liability protection. This can be particularly important if the SMSF owns real property
b. special purpose corporate trustees of an SMSF are entitled to discounted annual ASIC fees
c. in terms of what the auditor (and ultimately the Tax Office)

expects to see, the use of a special purpose corporate trustee results in significantly improved record-keeping and compliance

d from a succession planning perspective, it is significantly easier to regulate the control of a corporate trustee (by simply changing the directors from time to time) as opposed to that of individual trustees, where each time an individual trustee changes, there is often a mass of documentation to be prepared and notifications to be made

e in relation to sole member funds, the use of a corporate trustee significantly simplifies the overall structure of a SMSF, as a sole director company is permissible. In contrast, it is impossible to create a valid SMSF with an individual trustee and sole member because, in this instance, there must always be an additional individual who acts as a co-trustee.

Individual trustees

The nomination of successor trustees is important when a fund has individuals as trustees.

The retirement, resignation or death of an individual trustee might give rise to the need to transfer assets and arrange for bank account changes, unlike a company that has perpetual succession.

Some SMSFs have a founder or principal role vested in someone other than the members. This can be a powerful role as such a person may have the power to appoint or remove a trustee or vary the trust deed.

Is the trust deed up to date?

Difficulties can arise if an SMSF trust deed is not up to date and compliant with the law and planning strategies.

Any deficiency in the trust deed could result in there being substantial extra tax to pay, a severe lack of flexibility and possibly certain trustee decisions being rendered invalid. In an estate-planning context, some of the issues that should be considered include whether:

a the deed permits the making of a binding nomination
b there are any restrictions in relation to binding nominations (assuming they are permitted) – for instance, whom they may be paid to, whether the benefit is to be paid as a lump sum or as a pension, or whether there are time limits within which the death benefit is to be paid
c the deed permits a broad range of benefit options, including lump sum benefits, pensions and a mixture of both. The deed should also authorise reversionary pensions – that is, allowing the member's pension to be paid to the member's dependants upon the member's death
d the deed complies with current legislative provisions
e the deed allows for individual and/or corporate trustees, as desired
f benefits can be paid out in kind
g in kind contributions can be made
h eligible spouse contributions can be made.

Generally, in the absence of the need to be prescriptive in specific areas, SMSF trust deeds should be drafted so as to be as flexible as possible.

Age of trust deed

The age of the trust deed is generally a significant determinant of whether it should be updated. Specifically, there are some critical dates which, if the trust deed were established, or the most recent amendment occurred, prior to that date then serious consideration should be given as to whether the trust deed needs updating.

The superannuation system, as a whole, changed considerably with the introduction of the *Superannuation (Industry) Supervision Act 1993* (**SIS Act**). Generally speaking, trust deeds established prior to that date should be updated. SMSFs which still have trust deeds executed prior to that date raise additional concerns about how the fund can have obtained a notification that it is a complying fund – that is, a fund that complies with the provisions of the SIS Act and which requires an election by the fund trustee that the SIS Act applies to the SMSF.

Further significant amendments to the SIS Act were made in 2003 with, among other things, the introduction of the co-contribution rules.

Spouse contribution splitting was introduced on 1 January 2006 before the simplified super reforms came into force on 1 July 2007. The simplified super changes were arguably the most comprehensive changes since the introduction of the SIS Act and included:

a changes to the taxation of eligible termination payments
b changes to the payment of death benefits
c the abolition of reasonable benefit limits and the introduction of the contributions caps.

Pensions and commutation

When reviewing the pension and commutation provisions of a deed, ideally the terms of a trust deed should be as flexible as possible and allow the payment of all types of pensions.

Some older deeds are particularly prescriptive in relation to the payment of pensions; this appears to have arisen on the basis that the SIS Regulations require that the rules for the payment of each type of pension ensure that certain prescribed conditions are met.

The prescriptive approach seems to have been adopted in older deeds as it was assumed that, if the rules for the payment of each type of pension were not set out clearly in the trust deed, and pensions were not paid in accordance with these rules, the requirement to ensure that pensions were paid in a particular way could not be met and the SIS Regulations would be contravened.

However, the governing rules of an SMSF include not only the terms of the trust deed but also any rules contained in other documentation and any unwritten rules.

Therefore, the more modern approach is to have the pension provisions in the trust deed drawn as flexibly as possible.

Reserves

In relation to reserve accounts, it is generally recommended that the trust deed provide for the creation of reserve accounts. This is particularly important in relation to excess contributions.

Death benefit nominations

Many older trust deeds contain a provision that a binding nomination will lapse after a specific period of time (generally three years) or that a binding nomination can only be made in favour of a particular class of persons – for example, the member's legal personal representative – and not in favour of an individual.

Ideally, these provisions should be crafted as flexibly as possible and left to the discretion of the member at the time of making the binding nomination to place restrictions on their nomination, rather than to have a trust deed that prescribes particular restrictions.

'Hard-wired' binding nominations

There may also be cases where a member's binding nomination is hard-wired into the deed itself, rather than contained in the more usual form of a separate nomination addressed to the trustee and given by the member.

When drafting or reviewing a hard-wired binding nomination it is important to ensure that, as well as the nomination itself, there are clauses that specifically state that:

a the clause containing the nomination cannot be changed; neither can any other clause that would invalidate the clause containing the nomination be changed, without the member's consent

b the clause containing the nomination cannot be changed; neither can any other clause that would invalidate the clause containing the nomination be changed, after the relevant member's death.

The main advantage of this approach is that it limits the possibility that the SMSF trustee might lose a binding nomination or, after the member's death, might read the trust deed to determine the method for paying the member's death benefit without being aware that the BDBN is in place.

Re-contribution strategy

ANY SAVINGS (AND any earnings on these savings) held within superannuation that are 'tax-free components' are able to be distributed tax-free on death.

Tax-free components include:

a non-concessional contributions (formerly referred to as 'un-deducted contributions'), where no tax deduction has been received in relation to amounts contributed (for example, contributions made from post-tax earnings)
b government co-contributions.

One strategy that was historically of benefit involved withdrawing the taxable component from superannuation and then re-contributing it as a non-concessional contribution, with the result that all benefits became tax-free and enabled the whole super benefit to be paid to non-dependants as a lump sum, tax-free on a member's death.

Since 1 July 2007, the usefulness of this strategy has been weakened because:

a any withdrawal from a SMSF on a lump sum basis must be made proportionately as between tax-free and taxable components. In other words, it is not possible to withdraw only the taxable component
b there are significant limitations placed on the ability to contribute tax-free components to superannuation, namely:
   (i) non-concessional contributions are limited to $540,000 every three years, where the member is under 65 years of age

(ii) non-concessional contributions are limited to $180,000 per year where the member is over 65 years of age and the member satisfies the work test

(iii) no contributions can be made once the member reaches 75 years of age.

Accelerating superannuation contributions

Particularly given the ongoing adjustments to the limits for concessional superannuation contributions, the way in which to maximise non-concessional contributions receive significant interest.

Historically, the main strategies available in relation accelerating contributions have been best exemplified by the following table:

Member age	61	62	63	64	65	Total Contribs
Financial year	2013/14	2014/15	2015/16	2016/17	2017/18	
Scenario 1	$150,000	$150,000	$150,000	$150,000	$150,000[1]	$750,000
Scenario 2	$150,000	$150,000	$450,000	nil	nil	$750,000
Scenario 3	$150,000	$150,000	$150,000	$450,000	nil	$900,000
Scenario 4	$450,000	nil	nil	$450,000	nil	$900,000
Scenario 5	$150,000	$450,000	nil	nil	$450,000[2]	$1,050,000
Scenario 6	$150,000	$150,000	$150,000	$150,000	$450,000[1]	$1,050,000

In relation to the above table (and the further table below) it is important to note the following assumptions:

a contributions are made prior to member's 65th birthday or made after reaching age 65 and the member continues to satisfy the required gainful employment test.

b contributions are made prior to member's 65th birthday or the member was aged 65 at any time in the year and continues to satisfy the required gainful employment test and the contributions were made after the member's 65th birthday.

Changed thresholds commenced on 1 July 2014 and an updated version of the table, is set out below.

The updated table assumes that the first contribution is made after 1 July 2014.

If a combined contribution is commenced before 1 July 2014, the previous table continues to apply until the accelerated approach is completed.

Member age	61	62	63	64	65	Total Contribs
Financial year	2014/15	2015/16	2016/17	2017/18	2018/19	
Scenario 1	$180,000	$180,000	$180,000	$180,000	$180,000[1]	$900,000
Scenario 2	$180,000	$180,000	$540,000	nil	nil	$900,000
Scenario 3	$180,000	$180,000	$180,000	$540,000	nil	$1,080,000
Scenario 4	$540,000	nil	nil	$540,000	nil	$1,080,000
Scenario 5	$180,000	$540,000	nil	nil	$540,000[2]	$1,260,000
Scenario 6	$180,000	$180,000	$180,000	$180,000	$540,000[1]	$1,260,000

An alternative strategy that has developed is the establishment of an additional SMSF to receive all non-concessional contributions (tax-free components) so that, upon the member's death, the whole super benefit is paid to non-dependants, with the vast majority of that benefit being tax-free (although any earnings from investing the tax-free component are taxable). For example, the member could contribute any pension payments received or any after-tax amounts to the newly established SMSF.

Borrowing

Finally, in relation to borrowing, the trustee of an SMSF is prevented from borrowing money or maintaining an existing borrowing, unless the trustee complies with provisions of section 67A of the SIS Act.

It is important to note that, notwithstanding the borrowing might otherwise comply with the limited recourse borrowing provisions in section 67A of the SIS Act, there must be a specific power for the trustee to borrow, contained in the trust deed.

Furthermore, most financiers will require a number of other specific powers in the trust deed including:

a the power to grant the security for the borrowing
b the power to instruct the trustee of the trust which is to hold the asset that is the subject of the borrowing
c the ability for the SMSF trustee to be indemnified out of the assets of the SMSF, in the event the financier takes action
d the ability to accept various types of contributions, which will be used by the SMSF trustee to make the repayments on the borrowing
e the power to grant a power of attorney to provide to the financier the ability to act on behalf of the fund, in the event of default.

Anti-avoidance rules

IT IS IMPORTANT to note that when taxation issues are considered, as part of deciding how best to implement a specific transaction or wider arrangement, there is a risk that the ATO might review the transaction or arrangement and apply the general anti-avoidance rules contained in part IVA of the Tax Act.

Very broadly, part IVA may apply to the superannuation arrangements summarised above where it can be objectively determined, from all the circumstances, that the dominant purpose of any party to the transaction or arrangement, or to a part of the transaction or arrangement (Scheme), is to obtain a tax benefit for that party or another party associated with the Scheme.

The ATO must make a specific determination that part IVA applies. The ATO can then cancel the tax benefits otherwise obtained, reconstruct the transaction or arrangement for tax purposes and issue assessments, including penalties and interest relating to the disallowed tax benefit.

The interpretation of part IVA is highly technical and its application in each case requires a detailed consideration of the current case law and all the relevant facts. Unless a binding ruling under part IVA is obtained from the ATO, it is not possible to provide certainty about its possible application.

Chapter 4

PRIVATE TRUST ASSETS

What is a trust?

TRUSTS ARE AMONG the most popular investment and business vehicles available.

As explained in Chapter 1, a trust is created when a person (the trustee) holds property for the benefit of another person or persons (the beneficiaries).

The trustee is the legal owner of the property, but has an equitable obligation to hold the property for the benefit of others (being the beneficiaries), who may enforce such an obligation.

Usually, the obligation is expressed in writing, in the form of a trust deed. In administering a trust, the trustee must follow the terms of the trust deed.

The term 'trust' encompasses the whole relationship between the trustee and the beneficiaries in relation to the trust property. There is a vast range of different classes of trusts, including fixed trusts, unit trusts, hybrid trusts, discretionary (family) trusts and TTs.

How are trusts created?

Inter vivos Trusts

An *inter vivos* trust is a trust that is established by a person during that person's lifetime.

Assets may be transferred to the trust during the life of the person who has set up the trust, or after their death.

Where assets are transferred to the trust prior to the death of the testator, then they will not form part of the testator's estate.

An *inter vivos* trust is usually established by a trust deed, which sets out the terms of the trust.

TTs

A TT is a trust that is established by someone's will. As such, it is only activated upon the death of the testator.

As TTs are established by the will, the will serves as the trust deed.

A TT normally gives the trustee a wide discretion as to the distribution of the capital and income of the trust to the nominated beneficiaries.

TTs retain all the benefits of an *inter vivos* discretionary trust, but also provide greater levels of asset protection and tax planning.

A TT can also be established post-death for the purposes of receiving property from a deceased person's estate.

Who are the parties to a trust?

The settlor

The settlor is the person who first establishes the trust. Therefore, in a TT, the settlor is the will-maker.

The settlor is the person who has provided the initial trust property to the trustee, subject to the terms and conditions set out in the trust deed.

Normally, the settlor is not a beneficiary, and will not (after the creation of the trust) have any control over the trust.

It is common practice that a small initial amount is settled to establish the trust.

Settlement sums

The consequences of a failure to deposit the settlement sum on the establishment of a discretionary trust can be complex; however, the conservative position is that the settlement sum should always be deposited into the trust's bank account and, ideally, it should be the first deposit.

The placing of the settlement cheque (or a cash equivalent of it) on the file for the trust can be a problematic approach for a range of reasons, including:

a where the settlement sum is paid by cheque, the cheque will normally go stale after 13 months
b even when cash is stored with the trust, it is difficult to provide documentary evidence of the settlement sum forming part of the trust if the cash is lost.

Ensuring that the settlement sum is deposited into the bank account of the trust avoids both of these issues.

The trustee

The trustee is the person who holds and administers the property of the trust on behalf of the beneficiaries. The trustee controls the day-to-day operations of the trust.

There can be more than one trustee, but no more than four – in which case they act together to administer the estate. If one of the trustees dies, the remaining individuals will continue in their role.

A company can also act as a trustee.

The beneficiaries

The beneficiaries are those people who may benefit from the trust, either in the form of income distributions or capital distributions.

The beneficiaries under a trust can be individually named, or can come from a class of beneficiaries.

If a class of beneficiaries is nominated, the class must be sufficiently well defined so that it is clear who the beneficiaries are.

Who are beneficiaries under a trust deed?

The meaning of 'beneficiary', from a tax perspective was confirmed by the Federal Court in the case of *Yazbek v Federal Commissioner of Taxation* [2013] FCA 39.

The decision confirms that a 'beneficiary' is not simply a person who, as a matter of fact, has obtained some tangible benefit from the trust; rather a beneficiary is someone who is entitled to enforce the trustee's obligation to administer the trust according to its terms.

A comprehensive review of a trust deed should always include an analysis of every variation or resolution of a trustee or other person that might have an impact on the interpretation of the range of potential beneficiaries.

Some examples of documents that might have such impact on the class of potential beneficiaries are:

a resolutions of the trustee to add or remove beneficiaries pursuant to a power in the trust deed
b nominations or decisions of persons nominated in roles such as principal, appointor or nominator
c consequential changes triggered by the way in which the trust deed is drafted – for example, beneficiaries who are potential beneficiaries only while other named persons are living.

The trustee's duties

The trustee must deal with the trust assets for the benefit of the beneficiaries. In doing so, the trustee has a number of duties, namely:

a to carry out the terms of the trust, subject to the terms and conditions of the trust deed
b to preserve the assets of the trust, including insuring those assets
c to act impartially and in good faith, for the benefit of the beneficiaries named under the trust
d to exercise reasonable care in the administration of the trust; this means that the trustee should take all the steps and precautions that they would take in managing their own affairs
e to avoid any conflicts of interest
f to keep proper accounting records.

Void trusts

A number of consequences can flow from establishing a discretionary trust that does not have any default provisions that apply for the distribution of capital.

The issues in this regard are quite complex; however the conservative position is clear – that is, every discretionary trust should ideally have clear provisions that apply for the distribution of capital, in the event that a trustee fails to make a valid distribution.

The position in relation to default provisions for income is not so clear; where there are no fallback provisions for income, an undistributed amount will often form part of the capital of the trust.

Particularly following the High Court's decision in Bamford, many advisers now focus on all of the core provisions of their client's trust deeds; the absence of a default distribution of capital or, in some instances, a purported default distribution that does not operate effectively, is a trigger for minimising, at least, the assets that are acquired in a trust from that point onwards.

Another issue that arises relatively regularly is when the vesting day for the trust passes and, unfortunately, neither the client nor the adviser has realised it.

The questions of how exactly the income and capital of a trust should have been dealt with over the years since the trust ended and what the trust law issues, liability issues, tax issues and stamp duty issues are, normally are complex and often create significant expense.

How long can a trust continue to exist?

SOME TRUSTS, SUCH as charitable trusts, some superannuation funds and (potentially) trusts established under South Australia law, can continue indefinitely. However, most trusts must cease at some point in time and cannot continue for an indefinite period.

The trust deed generally sets out how long a trust is to last, and at what point the income and assets of the trust will be distributed.

However, a trust deed is subject to the law in relation to perpetuities, which, except in South Australia, prevents a trust from existing longer than 80 years.

The day on which the trust ends is called the vesting date.

When the trust ends, the assets remaining in the trust, plus any income historically accumulated, must be distributed to the beneficiaries by the trustee.

No assets must be left in the trust, and the trust must not continue to exist.

What happens to trust assets when the main decision-maker dies?

TRUST ASSETS ARE not governed by a testator's will. Unless the trust deed makes specific provision for the distribution of assets upon the death of a particular person, the trustee or replacement trustee will make that decision.

Usually, the trust deed will provide for replacing a deceased trustee.

Many trust deeds provide for a principal (also referred to as an appointor, guardian, protector or nominator) who has the power unilaterally to appoint or remove a trustee.

What is a family discretionary trust?

A FAMILY DISCRETIONARY TRUST is a trust where the trustee is given wide powers to determine which beneficiaries should receive the income and capital from the trust, and when that distribution should occur.

In a discretionary trust, the beneficiaries do not have any right to distributions of income or capital; such distributions occur at the trustee's discretion.

The trustee is also given discretion as to the types of investments that may be made, on behalf of the beneficiaries.

Ordinarily, the beneficiaries in a family discretionary trust are immediate family members, as well as brothers, sisters, cousins or any associated family companies.

It is common for family businesses to be conducted through discretionary trusts.

Lineal descendant trusts

'Lineal descendant trusts' come in many shapes and forms.

This type of structure has been popular, not only in recent years, but since trusts were established as asset protection and tax-planning vehicles in early English law.

In considering the establishment of such a trust (or reviewing a pre-existing trust), it is critical to understand how the legal firm involved in crafting the document has approached the task.

Some common themes in the structure of this kind of trust include:

a providing that income distributions be fully discretionary amongst both lineal and non-lineal descendants, with capital able to be distributed only to lineal descendants

b. both income and capital distributions being limited to lineal descendants
c. income and capital distributions being limited to lineal descendants, unless otherwise approved by, for example, the principal.

What role does the principal play in a family discretionary trust?

As noted above, the principal of a trust is the person nominated in the trust deed as having the power to appoint or remove a trustee.

Generally, this power of appointment and removal is a discretionary power and can be exercised at any time.

Therefore, the principal has a great deal of control over the trust, as they effectively control the trustee, who in turn controls the assets of the trust.

In some trust deeds, the power of appointment is flexible, and the current principal is able to nominate who will succeed them.

In other deeds, however, a successor principal may be specified or the power may end on the death or incapacity of the nominated principal.

When an individual trustee or principal dies, who takes over these functions?

IT IS IMPORTANT to look firstly at the particular trust deed to determine who will succeed as principal or trustee in the event of death.

If a trust deed nominates who is to succeed as a principal, then that person will become the new principal of the trust, and will be able to determine when to remove and replace trustees.

It may be possible for an existing principal to appoint a new principal via their will, but only if the trust deed allows this to occur.

On the death of the last surviving individual trustee, the executors of that person's estate will become the trustees of the trust, unless the trust deed provides otherwise.

Where the role of trustee or principal is held by a company, who gains control when a director or shareholder dies?

WHERE THE TRUSTEE is a company, the will-maker should have dealt with their shares in that company in their will.

The person who receives the shares will then effectively gain control of the company, as the shareholders have the power to appoint the directors and, in turn, the trust.

Again, this conclusion is subject to any powers of a principal of the trust.

Family trust deed updates

Since 2010, there have been several changes to the laws relating to the taxation of trusts. In summary:

a an announcement in December 2010 to rewrite the trust tax rules, in response to the *Bamford* decision
b an announcement in March 2011 to amend the rules relating to trust income and taxable income and deal with the streaming of capital gains and dividends
c a further announcement in the middle of April 2011 by the Government, changing its position so that the proposed rules would only deal with 'streaming' capital gains and dividends by 30 June 2011;

d legislation was subsequently amended dealing with streaming capital gains and dividends applicable for 30 June 2011 and onwards
e there is currently consultation taking place regarding the re-writing of the trust tax rules to align trust income and taxable income.

Generally speaking, therefore, trust deeds should be reviewed and possibly updated in the light of the above changes, for issues such as:

a powers to clarify the treatment of unpaid distributions to beneficiaries
b powers clarifying the trustee's ability to hold amounts as loans or unpaid entitlements
c amendments to the income definitions to clarify the trustee's power to re-characterise receipts
d permitting the trustee to rely on the concessions concerning the timing of when resolutions for distributions need to be made
e additional powers of the trustee and related provisions to improve the administrative efficiency of the trust, including powers to permit the trust to be cloned or split.

As the government has flagged that there are likely to be further changes in the area of trusts, there is a risk that any updates performed before the rewriting of the tax rules, mentioned above, is complete might need to be revisited at some point in the short to medium term.

Having said this, given that most trusts will not have been reviewed for many years (if at all), there are often significant benefits derived from proceeding with updates at this point.

Ultimately, it is important to undertake a 'general health check' of any trust – on a regular basis and certainly as part of an estate planning exercise. Broadly, a standard 'health check' should consider the following issues:

a the vesting day of the trust
b default beneficiaries of the trust

c. the day by which trust distribution resolutions must be made (for example, 30 June or such later time as may be allowed at law)
d. the definition of trust income – that is, what will be taken to be 'income of the trust estate', however described
e. powers to alter the meaning of the trust income – for example, by determining which receipts are capital and which are income
f. powers to allocate expenses and costs against particular income or gains
g. powers to attribute particular types of income to particular beneficiaries
h. powers to amend the deed
i. prior year losses – for example, whether offset against capital or able to be recouped from current year trust income
j. ability to hold amounts on separate sub-trusts for beneficiaries or permit those funds to be intermingled with the trust funds
k. attribution and streaming powers.

Trust establishment 101

The case of *Aston (Aust) Properties Pty Ltd v Commissioner of State Revenue* highlights how critical it is to ensure that new structures are established correctly.

In this particular instance, the taxpayer was arguing that group land tax assessments were incorrect, due to the ownership of various landholdings being via separate trusts.

The trusts that were alleged to exist were prepared by the taxpayer himself and he gave evidence that he had '*become convinced that the process of creating multi tiered trust structures could be undertaken in an efficient manner without the need to purchase off the shelf trust deeds from solicitors*'.

For many reasons the court held that the grouped land tax assessment was valid and that the purported trusts simply did not exist.

Some of the reasons why the court concluded that no trusts existed included:

a there was no evidence of any settlement sum being contributed on the initial creation of the trusts
b no evidence could be shown in relation to funds changing hands or to the creation of bank accounts
c while the trusts were purported to have been created via schedules that were recreated on numerous occasions, with reference to 'standard terms', the link to the standard terms could not be shown
d of the documents that could be produced, there was a significant number of errors and inconsistencies
e some transactions that had purportedly been entered into were by entities that did not exist.

What is a unit trust?

A UNIT TRUST IS a particular form of trust where the beneficial ownership is held through a specific number of units.

Unit holders subscribe to the trustee for units in the unit trust. A unit trust is governed by the same general principles as those for discretionary trusts – that is, there must be property vested in the trustee for the benefit of the beneficiaries. A unit trust can be diagrammatically represented as follows:

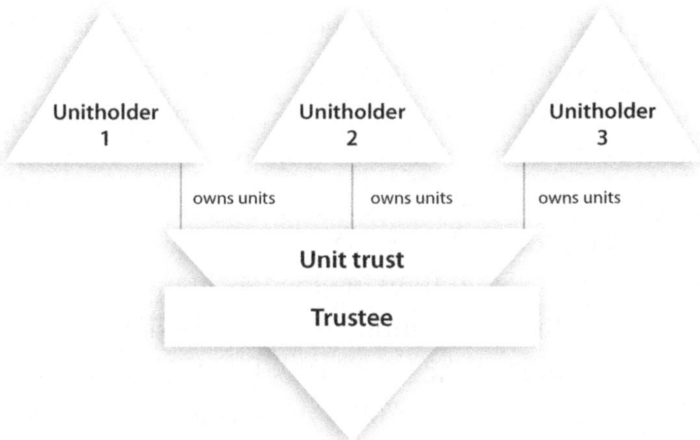

Generally, the trustee does not have discretion regarding the distribution of capital or income among the unit holders, unless units are of different classes with different rights attached to each class. For this reason unit trusts are often referred to as fixed trusts.

Care must be taken in using this term for tax purposes as fixed trusts have a specific definition under tax laws, and many unit trusts will not satisfy this definition. Whilst discretionary trusts confer on the trustee discretion as to the distribution of income or capital of the trust, the entitlement of beneficiaries of fixed and unit trusts depends on their fixed entitlement, or their unit holding.

Colonial decision

The decision in *Colonial First State Investments Limited v Commissioner of Taxation [2011] FCA 16* reinforces the position that the provisions of the trust deed are critical.

In brief terms, the key aspects of the decision were as follows:

a the main interest in the decision will be for the Australian funds management industry, as it focused on the tax effect of provisions in a unit trust that sought to allocate part of the taxable income to a unit holder redeeming units;

b the tests that must be satisfied to meet the definition of a 'fixed trust' for tax purposes will be difficult for many unit trusts. Here the unit trust was held not to constitute a fixed trust, primarily due to the wide amendment power that allowed changes to be made to unit holders' entitlements. The ability to satisfy the Tax Act definition of 'fixed trust' is important in a number of areas including:

   (i) to carry forward tax losses

   (ii) passing through franking credits to unit holders

   (iii) where superannuation funds are unit holders, avoiding application of the 'non-arm's length income' rules (note that prior to 1 July 2007, these rules were called 'special income');

c the attempt, by way of variation, to provide the trustee the discretion to allocate discounted and non-discounted capital gains to unit holders on redemption was ineffective.

The trustee has no discretion as to who may benefit from the trust, but the trustee has the same duties, obligations and liabilities as with any other trust.

Unit holders may be natural persons, companies or trustees for other (normally discretionary) trusts.

A unit trust is often used where people come together for a particular trading or property venture.

Many unit trusts are established to own and run a business, and often all the units in a unit trust are owned by a family discretionary trust to ensure some level of flexibility in dealing with the income and capital.

How can interests in the assets of a unit trust be transferred?

A PERSON'S WILL CANNOT deal with the underlying assets of a unit trust – only who is to receive the units that a will-maker individually owns.

The trust deed will determine what rights the unit holders have in relation to income and capital distribution.

It will also stipulate the rights of the unit holders when the trust is wound up.

What happens following the death of a person who owes money to a trust?

THE GENERAL RULE is that any debts owed at the time of a person's death must be repaid out of their estate.

This includes all moneys owed to a trust.

Therefore, it is important that all such loans and debts are documented, to ensure that the money can be recovered from the estate; further comments in this regard are set out below.

What happens following the death of a person who is owed money by a trust?

OFTEN TRUSTS DISTRIBUTE income to the beneficiaries, after which the income is loaned back to the trust. The distribution may be made, but left unpaid. A third alternative is that a beneficiary might have advanced into the trust capital that is yet to be repaid.

In each of the above situations, the outstanding amounts are debts owing to a will-maker at the time of their death and become an asset of that person's estate.

Unless there is an agreement in place, all debts are payable to the will-maker's estate at call. This means that if the estate so demands, the loan must be repaid immediately.

As part of an estate plan, therefore, a decision should be made as to where the will-maker wants the loan asset to go.

There are several options, including:

a allowing the loan to become part of the estate so that the beneficiary (or beneficiaries) who receives the residue (often a TT) will become entitled to repayment of the loan
b allocating the loan to a separate beneficiary
c having the loan repaid before death
d forgiving the loan.

There are potential tax and stamp duty consequences for each of the above approaches.

How are trusts taxed?

As a trust is not a separate legal entity, it is not itself taxed.

However, the trustee has the duty of lodging a tax return for the trust.

Beneficiaries who have received income and capital from the trust throughout each financial year must include those amounts in their own personal tax returns and are taxed in the usual way.

Where a beneficiary has received income, but is a minor, then the trustee is assessable for tax on that income as if it were the income of the trustee. Generally in relation to *inter vivos* trusts the tax rate for minors is the top marginal rate (plus Medicare).

Any undistributed funds are also included in the tax return completed by the trustee. Undistributed income is also taxed at the top marginal rate (plus Medicare) in the hands of the trustee.

Beneficiaries who have not received income from the trust are said to have a 'mere expectancy' of receiving income from the trust in the future. Accordingly, the trustee must pay tax on any undistributed income on the basis that no beneficiary is 'presently entitled'.

Chapter 5

ASSETS IN COMPANIES

What happens to company shares owned by the will-maker upon death?

UNLIKE A TRUST, a company is a separate legal entity. It has its own legal identity that is discrete from the shareholders.

Companies can own property, enter into contracts and be subject to legal liability in the same manner as an ordinary person.

Shares represent ownership of a company. However, even as owner, a shareholder is not entitled to the assets of the company. Thus, the death of a shareholder has no effect on the company's continuing existence.

However, the shares owned by the will-maker in a company form part of their estate assets and can be disposed of by their will.

During the period when the will-maker's estate is being administered, their executor will be able to exercise any rights that attach to their shares – for example, voting at general meetings.

Debts owed to the will-maker by the company

A COMPANY CAN OFTEN owe money to its shareholders. This may arise, for example, if shareholders lend the dividends they earn back to the company.

This sum then becomes an asset of the will-maker, separate from the shares themselves.

Ordinarily, it is expected that an individual will intend both their shares and the loan asset to go to the same person; however, the loan will make up part of the residuary estate if it is not specifically gifted.

In a similar way, as summarised above, for loans by will-makers to trusts, there are several options for will-makers who are owed money by a company, including:

a allowing the same beneficiary to receive both the shares in the company and the loan (either directly, or via a TT)
b allowing the loan to become part of the residuary estate, so that the beneficiary who receives the residuary estate becomes entitled to the loan
c allocating the loan to a separate beneficiary
d causing repayment of the loan prior to death
e forgiving the loan to the company.

Again, there is a range of potential tax and stamp duty consequences in relation to each of the above alternatives.

Debts owed by the will-maker to the company

A DEBT OWED BY the shareholder to the company ordinarily causes a debit loan account to arise.

There are several potential tax consequences when dealing with the debt (particularly under the deemed dividend rules in Division 7A of the Tax Act).

Practically, subject to managing the tax issues, any debt owed by a will-maker to a company, on death may be:

a repaid by the estate
b forgiven
c repaid prior to death
d allowed to form part of the estate, so that a beneficiary inherits the obligation to repay the debts.

Chapter 6

PARTNERSHIP ASSETS

What is a partnership?

A PARTNERSHIP IS A relationship that exists between persons carrying on a business in common with a view of profit.

Often there will be in place a partnership agreement that sets out the rights and obligations of the partners, particularly on death.

If there is a partnership agreement, its provisions will determine the conduct of the business and how the assets and liabilities (including tax) of the business are dealt with.

Where there is no agreement, the liabilities and obligations in partnerships are simply shared jointly between the partners.

A limited partnership is where one or more of the members have contributed capital to the business, but usually take no part in the management.

The limited partner is only liable for the debts of the partnership to the value of the capital contributed.

Limited partnerships

The use of limited partnerships to avoid Division 7A was an approach that the ATO was on record as having concerns about long before the legislation in this area was changed.

Following the change, a number of advisers were quick to realise that companies limited by guarantee could offer a similar pathway to the limited partnership approach; in other words:

a potentially receive trust distributions, with the tax payable on those distributions capped at the corporate rate of 30%
b the company limited by guarantee could then subsequently make loans that would not, on the face of the legislation, be caught by Division 7A.

In their taxpayer alert TA2011/1, the ATO lists its concerns relating to the above strategy.

What are the assets of the partnership?

Assets in a partnership can be held by the partners via a corporate or trust structure or individually.

The assets of a partnership may include:

a goodwill
b business assets, such as stock
c land or interests in land
d intellectual property
e shares in a company, or units in a unit trust.

What happens to partnership assets owned by the will-maker upon death?

WHEN AN INDIVIDUAL ceases to be part of a partnership, the partnership will usually be at an end, unless the partnership agreement provides otherwise.

This means that the deceased partner's executor has the right to demand that the value of the deceased partner's interest in the partnership be transferred to the estate.

If this occurs, the assets of the partnership might need to be sold in order for the outgoing partner's interest to be disposed of.

A partner can make provision in their will for the succession of their interest in the partnership, although any contrary agreements made while the partner is still alive will take precedence over the will.

It is important for all partners to determine whether they wish the partnership to continue on the exit of a partner and to make the appropriate provision in a partnership agreement.

If the partnership continues, the continuing partners will generally have the right to acquire the interest of the outgoing partner (or their estate).

An insurance funded buy-sell arrangement is often used to keep the partnership operating and to give the remaining partners an opportunity to acquire the outgoing partner's interest.

A practical guide to business succession is a complementary publication to this book and provides significant insight to the area.

Debts owed to the will-maker by a partnership

Debts that are owed to the will-maker by a partnership can include:

a loans made to the partnership
b unpaid distributions of partnership profit
c unpaid partnership management fees or salary.

How can debts be dealt with?

As is the case with debts owed by a company or trust, there are several options for debts owed to a partner on death, including:

a to leave the debts as they are, with the outgoing partner (or their estate) able to demand immediate repayment
b if the debts are currently on an informal basis, (that is, made on a handshake) to document the agreed terms in writing.

Obviously, however, even if there is a formal agreement, a repayment obligation on a partnership might cause financial hardship, particularly considering that the earning potential of the partnership might be reduced by the loss of a partner.

Debts owed by the will-maker to a partnership

Debts owed by a will-maker to a partnership usually arise due to loans made by the partnership to the partners.

They might also be advances against anticipated future drawings.

How can the debt be dealt with?

The options for debts owed by a partner include to:

a leave the debts as they are, with the partnership able to demand repayment from the estate of the deceased partner
b document the debts in writing
c take out insurance over the debts owed by the partner, so that the partnership can be fully repaid.

Flowchart for partnership succession planning

Chapter 7

BENEFICIARIES WITH PARTICULAR NEEDS

Providing for beneficiaries

IT IS IMPORTANT to remember, as part of a comprehensive estate plan, to provide adequately for all beneficiaries that might have special needs.

Tailored TTs can be used effectively to resolve some of the issues referred to below.

Giving a life-interest in various assets (also known as a life-tenancy), or a right to occupy can also be an effective strategy.

Rights to occupy

Traditionally, life estates were created where a will-maker wanted to allow a particular beneficiary the right to reside in a property without gifting it to them directly.

For many reasons, the creation of a life interest is rarely appropriate as part of a modern day estate plan, and generally the use of a specially crafted TT or a right to occupy are the appropriate approaches.

Some of the reasons that life estates are no longer of particular use include:

a a traditional life estate is very inflexible, particularly if the life tenant no longer wishes to reside in the property

b the original property might no longer be appropriate because of its size, its geographic location or because of the level of care required for the individual, who might, for example, need to move to a nursing home

c will-makers often craft the life estate so that it ends when the life tenant enters into a new spousal relationship; the courts have been clear that such a restriction is likely to be struck down as void

d there are several inflexibilities in relation to the way in which the life tenant and the remainderman can interrelate; ultimately, it is often very difficult to end the arrangements other than on the death of the life tenant

- there are significant adverse revenue consequences, both from a tax and stamp duty perspective, which can arise in relation to life estates. These difficulties are particularly detrimental if there is a desire to end the life estate before the death of the life tenant.

Has any beneficiary with an intellectual disability been adequately provided for?

The future needs of beneficiaries who have a disability need to be carefully considered.

Considerations will often include:

a the psychological and physical needs of the child, and the degree of dependency
b any young siblings who will also need to be provided for
c any siblings that may be able to be the trustee of the TT for the child with a disability
d the eligibility of the relevant person for a pension or other social security arrangements
e whether the special needs beneficiary has the ability to live in the family home and thus be granted a life tenancy or right of occupancy
f control of any *inter vivos* special disability trust.

There are numerous potential options to provide adequately for a beneficiary with a disability, which include:

a assets may be given directly to a person
b assets may be left via a TT for the benefit of the person. The income from the assets can be used to pay for the person's development, to ensure a steady income stream. The benefit of the TT can then be later given to other beneficiaries
c assets may be given or left on trust to a service organisation on the condition it provides long-term support for the person.

Have any elderly dependent parents been adequately provided for?

It is possible for the will-maker's parents to bring a claim for provision out of their child's estate, if they have been dependent on the will-maker and still need to be provided for.

The options for providing for elderly parents include:

a setting up a TT for one or both parents during their lifetime, with the control and benefit then passing to other beneficiaries
b a life interest or right to occupy in real estate could be provided.

Should a life tenant subsequently develop a need for nursing home accommodation, provision should be made for the house to be sold and the proceeds held on trust and applied for the purposes of meeting nursing home expenses.

Have any children from a previous relationship been adequately provided for?

IT IS IMPORTANT to make sure that any children from a previous relationship are provided for.

Often, the simplest approach is to set up a TT under the will for the purposes of funding the child's education and maintenance.

A gift could be left to the TT, with control given to the child absolutely when they attain a specified age.

Do any arrangements need to be made for a spendthrift or drug-dependent beneficiary?

If it is possible that a beneficiary's share of an estate might be lost through substance dependency or gambling difficulties, then steps should be taken to ensure the wealth is held via a specially crafted TT.

Under the terms of the TT, the beneficiary (and their family) could receive income from the TT only as reimbursement of approved expenses.

In this way, the capital is conserved for the next generation of the family, whilst still adequately providing for the at-risk beneficiary during their life.

Will sufficient funds be available to dependants between the will-maker's death and the distribution of the estate?

WHEN A FAMILY member dies, especially where that person is the primary income earner, there is often an urgent need for access to funds.

If an executor experiences a delay in obtaining probate and therefore a delay in distributing the assets of the estate, the will-maker's dependants could be left without sufficient funds to carry out basic day-to-day household activities.

A beneficiary's legal right in respect of the estate assets does not arise until the administration of the estate is complete. Until that time, a beneficiary has no title to any asset, and cannot demand to be given their interest in the estate.

Delays often occur, but this problem can be overcome by setting up at least one joint bank account during the will-maker's lifetime.

Then, if the surviving dependant requires funds, they can be accessed immediately following the will-maker's death.

Other options available to ensure that dependants have immediate access to funds to meet expenses and short term needs include:

a owning sufficient cash assets in respective names
b each owning a life policy on the other for a (relatively) nominal amount
c ensuring that some funds are paid directly to dependants – for example, a lump sum from a superannuation fund.

Chapter 8

CGT

Could CGT cause an unintentional imbalance in the distribution of the estate?

THE DISPOSAL OF assets pursuant to a will might have tax consequences that should be considered at the time the will is drafted.

Different categories of assets and beneficiaries will have different CGT characteristics and implications.

Firstly, it should be noted that CGT does not normally become payable on a simple distribution of a person's estate to beneficiaries in accordance with their will.

CGT does however become payable when the executor or beneficiary disposes of or otherwise deals with the asset.

Assets to which CGT does not apply

CGT should not apply to these assets:

a the will-maker's main residence – if it is sold within two years of their death
b the will-maker's main residence – if it is used by a beneficiary as their main residence under a right in the will (even if sold after two years)
c motor vehicles
d personal belongings not exceeding $10,000
e most superannuation and life insurance policies
f for small business owners, assets where all relevant CGT small business concession conditions are satisfied.

Cost base for CGT

Assets purchased by a will-maker before 19 September 1985 and which are transferred to a beneficiary under a will are deemed to have been acquired by the beneficiary at the market value at the time of the deceased's death.

Assets purchased by the will-maker after 20 September 1985 and later transferred to a beneficiary are deemed to have been acquired by the beneficiary at the deceased's cost base.

Residency

WHERE A BENEFICIARY is a non-resident or has lived overseas for two years or more, CGT is immediately payable on certain distributions made to them under an estate.

These distributions include overseas real estate, jewellery and shareholdings in a public company that are less than 10%.

Unless specifically provided for in the will, the estate may be required to pay the CGT.

Trust distributions to a non-resident beneficiary

Generally, withholding tax is payable on all dividends, interest or royalties included in the income paid by a resident trust to a non-resident beneficiary, to the extent that the non-resident beneficiary is presently entitled to the relevant amount.

For example, if a resident trust validly distributes income to beneficiaries in the United States (who are non-resident beneficiaries), then:

a under the withholding tax system, a flat rate of tax is deducted from the source of the income before the income is sent overseas

b each part of the income (depending on whether it is interest, dividends or royalty distribution) will be taxed on the relevant withholding tax rate generally ranging between 10% and 15%

c often the beneficiary will not be subject to any other tax.

Importantly, however, with any trust distributions to non-residents where the withholding tax rules do not apply, the trustee will be taxed at the top marginal rate.

Capital gains tax and non-resident beneficiaries

Historically, non-resident individuals could access the 50% capital gains tax (**CGT**) discount on capital gains, on the disposal of Australian real property or shares in land rich entities, provided that there was an ownership period of more than 12 months.

However, for any capital gains made after 8 May 2012 by a non-resident disposing of a taxable Australian asset, regardless of whether the asset was owned by the individual or via a trust, there is no access to the 50% CGT discount.

The 50% CGT discount is still available for any capital gains accrued, but not crystallised, prior to 8 May 2012, although an independent valuation is likely to be required.

Trustees of trusts with non-resident beneficiaries will need to be particularly mindful of issues such as the following:

a having a mixture of capital gains on taxable and non–taxable property when distributing to a non-resident
b if a beneficiary becomes a non–resident after 8 May 2012 and the relevant asset disposed of was acquired prior to that date
c ensuring the benefit of accessing the 50% CGT discount on accrued gains as at 8 May 2012 by obtaining a valuation.

How can such an imbalance be rectified?

THE WILL-MAKER CAN deal with their assets while they are still alive by placing them in appropriate structures such as trusts or a company.

It might also be possible to utilise some of the numerous CGT rollover concessions available. The control of the trust or company can then be passed pursuant to the will without triggering any CGT liabilities.

If this type of alternative is not suitable, a TT may be set up in the will in order to structure the future ownership of the assets in a way that delays any CGT liability, potentially indefinitely.

To avoid inequality in distributions caused by CGT, the will-maker may give their executor specific powers to value the assets of the estate and to make distributions, taking into account reductions or increases in the value of the assets because of CGT.

The will-maker should consider carefully how to set out any specific gifts and to specify where the CGT will be paid from – that is, from the residue or from the gift itself.

Have sufficient records of assets been kept for CGT purposes?

Will-makers are required to maintain records of the purchase price and date of purchase of all CGT assets acquired on or after 20 September 1985.

The type of information that should be kept includes:

a the date of acquisition
b the cost of acquisition
c the cost of additions and alterations
d the date of disposal and the consideration.

Other CGT provisions

If a will requires the executor to purchase an asset in order to satisfy a specific legacy, it is accepted that the beneficiary is entitled to the asset from the time of its acquisition.

If a deceased's will provides for a legacy, and an asset is transferred by the executor in order to meet that legacy, then it will not amount to a disposal for CGT purposes, provided that the will contains a power of appropriation.

If, pursuant to the will, an option is granted to a beneficiary to purchase an asset of the estate, the ATO regards the exercise of the option as triggering a disposal. In that case, the beneficiary receives the property, not under the estate but rather as a purchaser under the option.

Where an executor simply sells assets to a beneficiary, this is regarded as a disposal by the executor and therefore taxable in the estate, for CGT purposes.

Where the beneficiaries under a will enter into a 'Deed of Arrangement' in settlement of a claim against the estate – such as a family provision application – the ATO accepts that any asset transfers to achieve the settlement are not taxable disposals. This is notwithstanding that under the will the beneficiary might not have had any entitlement to the asset.

Chapter 9

WHERE TO START

Arguably, the most important aspect of an estate planning exercise is understanding the factual matrix. In most situations, a methodical approach, using tables and diagrams, represents best practice.

Set out below is a description of a set of circumstances, followed by suggested tables and diagrams, which summarise the factual situation.

The facts

Jim (60) and Joy (59) are married and have three children: Maureen (38), Amanda (37) and Paul (35).

Paul is currently married to Kylie and they have three children together: Sam (5), Ben (3) and Josh (1). Paul also has a child, Kate (14), from a previous relationship.

Jim and Joy own, in their own names, a family home worth approximately $1,200,000 and there is a loan owed to Jim from the Robertson Family Trust of $800,000.

Jim and Joy act as trustees of the Robinson Super Fund. The SMSF owns listed shares of approximately $2,400,000 and cash of approximately $300,000; the SMSF is the sole unit holder of the Robinson Property Trust, which holds a property worth approximately $850,000.

Separately, there is a discretionary trust (Robinson Family Trust) with a corporate trustee (J & J Robinson Pty Ltd). The trust is used as a trading trust and the shares in the corporate trustee are owned by Paul and Kylie (one share each). The assets and liabilities of the trust are summarised as follows:

a listed shares ($500,000)
b commercial building, from where the business is run ($1,400,000)
c coast unit ($1,200,000)
d an interest in a partnership ($1,000,000)
e an unpaid present to Robinson Investments Pty Ltd ($900,000).

Paul and Kylie have the following assets and liabilities:

a the family home, owned as joint tenants (market value of $1,200,000 with a liability of $700,000)
b investment property, in Paul's sole name (market value of $1,000,000 with a liability of $800,000)
c a loan owed to Paul from the Robinson Family Trust.

There are currently no life or disability arrangements.

Robinson Group

Family structure

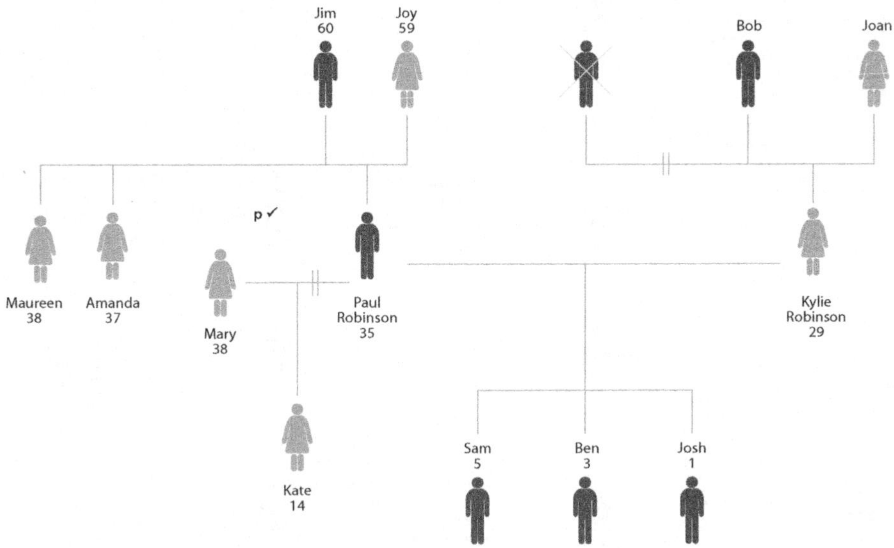

Key information for your personal estate plan

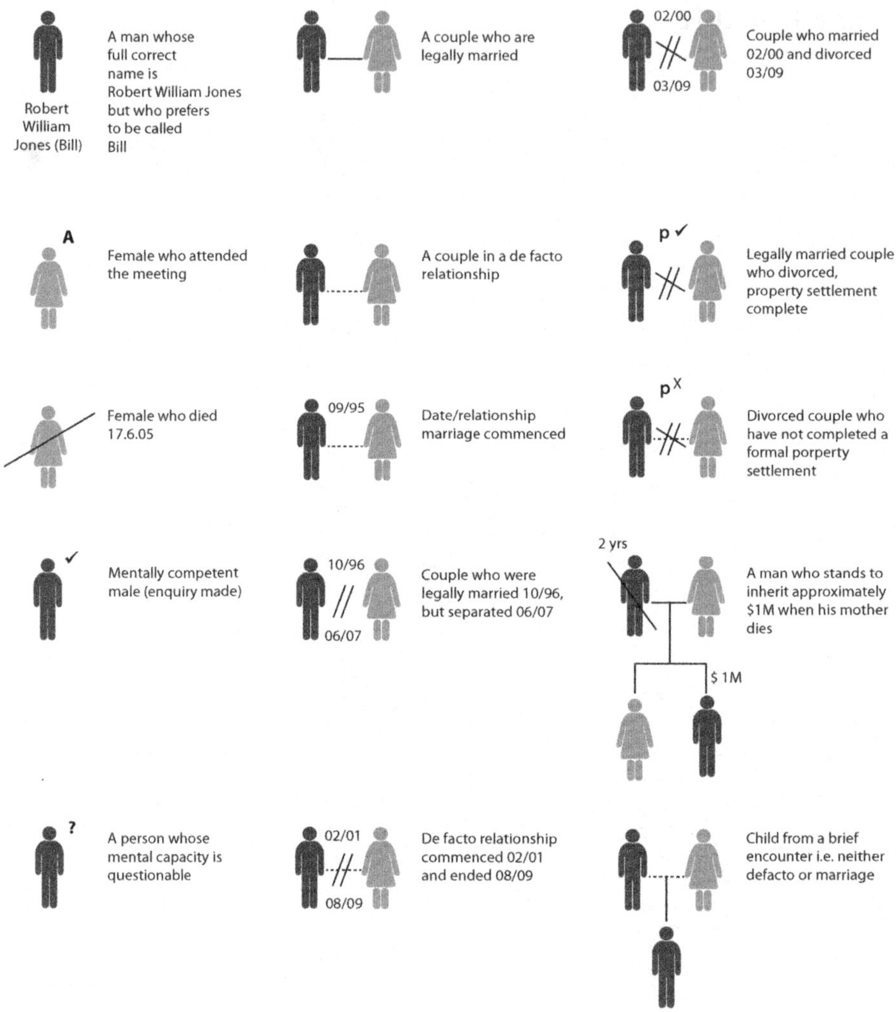

Robinson Group

Business Entities (existing structure)

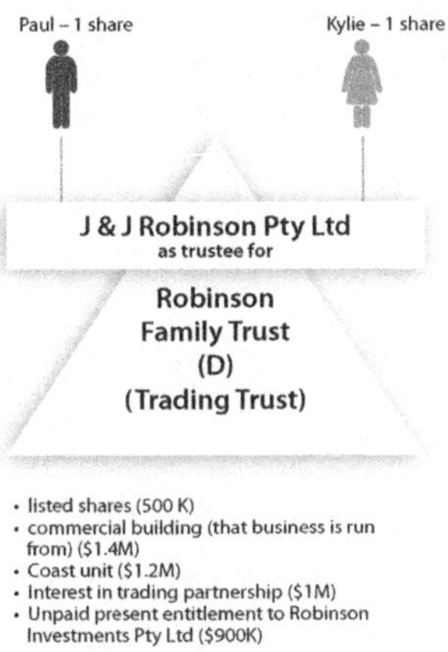

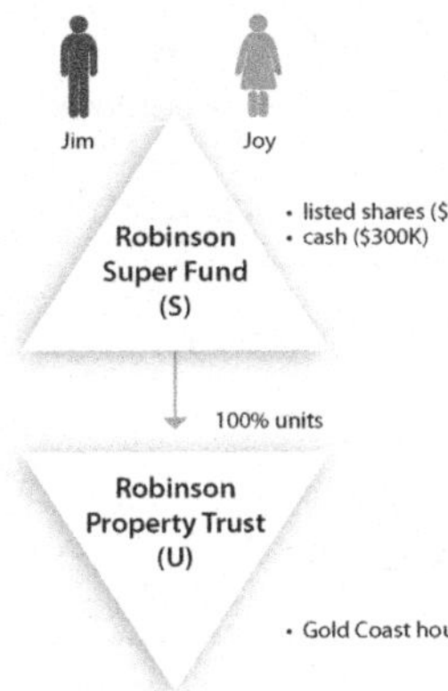

Assets	Market Value	Liabilities
Family home (joint tenancy)	$1,200,000	Nil
CR loan to Jim (Robertson Family Trust)	$800,000	
Net Assets	**$2,000,000**	

Assets	Market Value	Liabilities	Net value
Family home (joint tenancy)	$1,200,000	$700,000	$500,000
Investment property (Paul's name on title only)	$1,000,000	$800,000	$200,000
CR loan to Paul (Robertson Family Trust)	$300,000	Nil	$300,000
Net Assets	**$2,500,000**	**$1,500,000**	**$1,000,000**

Key information for your personal estate plan

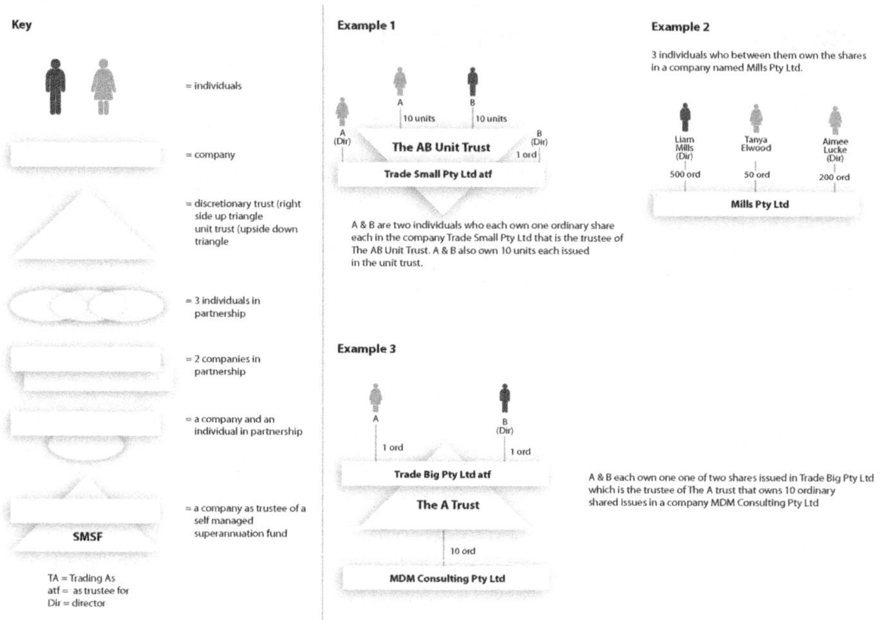

Made in the USA
Monee, IL
13 September 2026

62975579R00095